ISBN: 978-1-7321877-0-2

Under no circumstances should any material in this book be construed as an endorsement for and/or against any existing (or former) political candidates in elected office.

Thank You

This book is dedicated to my immediate family. It is also a tribute to those that shaped my development.

The following mentors are to be acknowledged:

Damian DeMarco, Jim McEvoy, Dave Brady, Ralph Nader[1], Congressman Amory Houghton[2], Duane Chapman, Tom Hirschl, Jon Conrad, Rob Miller, Jimmy Ohiro, Atomman Kimm, Keith Reed and Nan Miraglio.

1996 Photo of Matthew Myers, Intern for Congressman Amory Houghton with Ralph Nader.

---

[1] This photo is *not* a political endorsement of any kind.

[2] My work with Congressman Amory Houghton is also *not* a political endorsement; or a recommendation to vote along *any* political lines.

Table of Contents

Introduction

I sat down to write this during a year sabbatical that involved moving my parents across the country from California (along Route 66) to the South and then ultimately to settle in Connecticut. I have time to write this because I am currently providing elder care that presents its own challenges and complications. Time moves on. Capture the memories while you can.

This book combines macroeconomic analysis and technical business experienced in the real world along with my personal life's evolution. Volume 2 is already in the works.

The story behind this photo will be explained in Volume 2!

The Imperative Need to Fund Infrastructure Now

The time to fund infrastructure is now. The global backlog for public works has been determined to be $57 trillion by 2050. In the United States alone, there is a projected $3.7 trillion need for infrastructure improvements by 2020. This amount grows larger every day.

The current administration *must* come through with its promise to address this backlog.

This translates into substantial economic activity. However, the longer it takes to fund infrastructure initiatives in the present the more expensive they become in the future (in real dollars).

Where will the funding for these programs come from? They will require the cooperation of Federal, State and local governments, but most importantly they will necessitate that the private sector step forward to develop innovative solutions.

Technology can address these needs.

The current government (executive and legislative branches) has been unable to reach a consensus on funding these initiatives. They have failed to grasp the larger picture and remain *exceptionally myopic* in their short-term leadership.

Re-examining the infrastructure funding that President Franklin D. Roosevelt helped to build during the New Deal (which was expanded upon by President Dwight D. Eisenhower) provides a clear illustration of the significant multiplier effect that funding public works created: resulting in new jobs, businesses and innovation.

The projects that the Civilian Conservation Corps implemented in California and in the rest of the United States are impressive. Let's continue this activity in 2018 and beyond - and rollout similar programs that are tailored for today's world.

The United States needs a master plan for coordinated infrastructure. It requires shovel-ready programs that are *not* reactive but actively proactive, job creating and restorative.

Civilian Conservation Corps (CCC) was responsible for building bridges like the one featured in Big Sur, California.

Building Workplace Facilities and Infrastructure to Support Innovation

Bell Labs Innovation

From the late 1920s on, Bell Labs® produced some the world's most groundbreaking technologies: the transistor, the laser, the silicon solar cell, communication satellites, fiber optic cable systems, data networks, programming languages Unix and C, in addition to all of AT&T's® technological support for its nationwide networks.

What was the critical element that drove this innovation? : Mervin Kelly and his building's *infinite halls* at Bell Labs. These were designed to extend beyond the eye's focus and reach, but their usage forced scientists, engineers, chemists, and researchers to collide in the halls. The research resulted in creating an explosion of technology that provided the basis for the computers and data networks that we use today.

Fast forward to 2018, this model *must* be replicated across other private sector organizations, governmental and the civic spaces that the public operates in.

Why?

It is because many of the world's most complex problems can be solved by designing architectural and civic spaces that force people to *collide* in real-time, *not* via email or teleconference.

Computers and their computational overlay will not disappear.

However, it is the interaction of people through architecture using science and technology that will solve problems, not technology alone dictating how people will innovate.

Take some of the California's most pressing problems: its dire water shortage, housing problems and need to create a sustainable manufacturing base. Similar challenges that the nation faces can be addressed by creating civic and corporate spaces that require people to interact through architecture.

Neighborhoods have exploded with growth after expressways that had divided them have been *removed* - thereby creating new corridors for civic interaction and business. Highway I-195's relocation to the outskirts of Providence, Rhode Island is doing just this.

We must move quickly to build infrastructure and architecture that will support innovation, not stifle it.

This can be accomplished by creating the *infinite halls* of the future.

Organizational Network Mapping and Designing the Society of the Future

Introducing Organizational Network Mapping

Network Mapping involves the use of computerized models to study how people interact in companies. It examines who the *connectors* are in the workplace, even if they are not defined on traditional organizational charts as assuming these roles.

There is an extensive amount of literature written about studying and documenting this connectivity in corporate cultures. The maps that are produced as a result of these studies look like spider-webs, outlining the central hubs and outliers within a company, government agency or community not-for-profit.

To provide real world context, in a previous professional role, one of these *influencers* was a charismatic planner. She was the *glue* of the agency injecting humor into a largely static group of engineers. Although her role was limited to being a project manager in the hierarchy, she enabled people and information to flow between her and other members of the network.

How did this occur?

Visitors to the office, engineers and planners, and other employees would congregate at her desk due to its central location in the office. They would exchange news and discuss upcoming projects there before heading back to their desks. This *hub* had a positive disruptive effect on the team. It forced these engineers to interact offline and actually increased their productivity.

A visual delineation of the group would have shown this planner and her desk as the center of organization with the majority of the office radiating to and from her desk.

Why is this observation important?

Network maps are very valuable for managers to work to improve the efficiency of their operations and draw *outliers* closer to center. Perimeter employees typically have an extensive amount of valuable information and skill-sets that are being under-utilized by an organization.

It also suggests that this specific planner's role should have been redefined and expanded, elevating and promoting her into a more senior managerial role.

Extending Organizational Mapping Outside of Individual Corporations and Into Society

While much has been written about how to increase the efficiency and productivity of corporations through plotting, there is very little discussion of how to represent and document interlinks between two corporations, other government branches, community groups or NGOs.

A diagram that documented who *the connectors* were between two corporations (or between a government agency and a company) would be extremely valuable. These individuals might be two product managers (one at the corporation and another at a government role) who have lunch together on most afternoons.

Beginning to document and chart these connections can create more efficient environments, because roadblocks can be identified and circumvented. Once these barriers have been removed information can flow more freely between two agencies.

Roles can then be redefined in an organization, advancing these team members to managerial (and principle) negotiators within their respective companies.

Solving Societal Problems

Network mapping can be used to begin to solve some of the most complex societal problems, by defining who the connectors are in their communities and in their professional roles.

Blockades can be pinpointed and by-passed.

In the case of elected officials, these barricades may be occurring due to excessive amounts of campaign contributions by lobbyists.

Removing these *elected officials* and replacing them with new ones could provide the disruptive action that is necessary to move an important public works project forward. Effective diagraming can identify the connections between elected officials and corporations that are causing valuable projects to be sidelined or stalled.

A network portrayal of the lobbying agencies (representing corporations) that have contributed to U.S. Presidential, Senatorial and Congressional (or local) political campaigns can be used to document why essential infrastructure projects have not been initiated. This includes the replenishing of the Highway Trust Fund through increasing the gasoline tax; and/or providing some alternative means of underwriting essential national road construction or repair projects.

Most importantly a network portrayal can be used to delineate what the roadblocks to modernizing the nation's crumbling infrastructure are.

The Future is Mobile

Infrastructure Upgrade, Inc.®[3] has developed mobile applications to address real-world problems, including those that our communities face. IUI® provides professional architects, engineers and planners with sophisticated tools to solve their most complex job-site and planning issues.

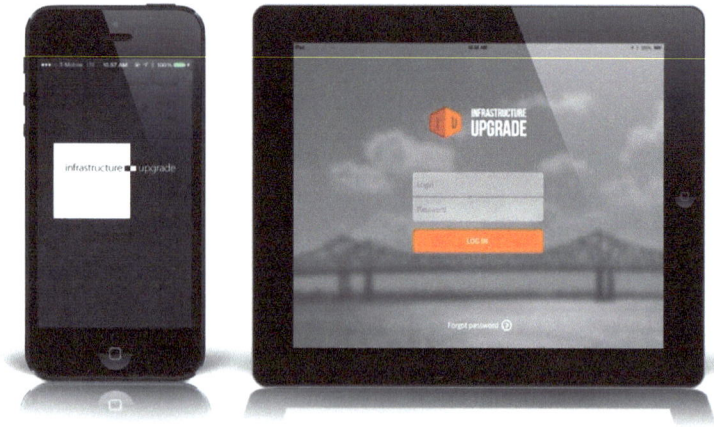

Apple®, Google® (Android®) and Microsoft® mobile devices can operate in remote locations and construction sites

---

[3]These are located at www.iuienterprise.com and www.infrastructureupgrade.com.

taking the power of cloud computing that was once confined to desktop applications into the field.

Desktop applications and enterprise systems will *not* disappear. However, traveling to the field provides context to a project: what surrounds it, how people interact in the area, and the problems that need to be addressed. Site visits are an extremely valuable method of pinpointing issues, including those identified on a new housing project, fiber optic installation or other construction project.

Mobile applications allow users to document concerns that they observe in real-time.

This is a powerful advancement that will shape both the future of computing and professional service organizations using electronic applications.

The *future* is mobile.

Matthew L. Myers, CEO and Founder of Infrastructure Upgrade, Inc.® at Techmanity® in San Jose, California.

Infrastructure to Support Commuters and the Modern Workplace

Disrupting the Commute and the Car

Much has been said about driverless cars, ride-sharing platforms, on-demand cabs and mobile applications that increase the speed and efficiency of your commute.

They *all* have a place.

However, has any technology been invented in one hundred plus years that actually disrupts the automobile?

As the average American sits in traffic for their morning commute, crawling along at 5 to 15 miles an hour in six to seven lanes of traffic each way, they must begin to wonder what is the purpose of the two to three hours that they spend each day to commuting to work? There are only so many e-books, songs to listen to and telephone calls that can be made.

A person's health begins to suffer sitting in a sedentary position all day.

For the average worker this inactivity includes: (1) watching television at breakfast; (2) in a car for another hour plus to commute to work; (3) working at a desk at a computer; (4) in a car on the way home; (5) jumping on the computer again after dinner; and (6) finally sitting to watch television or read before going to bed.

There is one invention (already in place) that has been left out of this discussion. To this day it is one of the most efficient machines that engineers have ever produced.

It doesn't require as much energy to manufacture or operate as a car.

It is compact and easy to store in your apartment, condo or house.

It requires minimal infrastructure, reducing upfront financing, underwriting and maintenance costs. It doesn't require twelve lanes of expressway to utilize. In San Francisco you can take it on BART and other public transportation.

It actually improves your health. This is particularly important with health and obesity reaching epidemic levels in the United States and the world, costing everyone billions of dollars in increased insurance and health care costs.

It increases productivity in the workplace, reducing stress and providing clarity of thought.

It doesn't cost up to $10,000 per year to maintain. Instead maintenance costs average around $100 + a year.

The answer is simple: the bicycle.

Cycling generates **camaraderie** amongst participants, creating tangible goals and socialization.

Creating a Different Corporate Culture

At Infrastructure Upgrade, Inc. (IUI)® we are disrupting the car's dominance. IUI supports a workplace that does not rely solely on one of the world's greatest monopolies: the automobile.

The author regularly commutes via bicycle (both on and off the road), logging 3,000 + miles so far this year. Join me and other IUI® team members on the road.

The personal pictures above were taken on Oʻahu and Mauʻi, Hawaiʻi, British Columbia, Canada and California, including the 36 mile Cycle to the Sun race up Haleakela, Mauʻi.

Matthew Myers dirt jumping in a private location.

Efficient Infrastructure and Removing Toxicity in Society

The rise of social media has connected the world through technology. However, it has created platforms filled with toxicity, reducing discussion, debate and civilized discourse. Intermodal systems that connect communities (rather than dividing them) and force people to interact while being physically fit have the following effect: they reduce toxicity and medical costs.

Jump off your chair, desk, couch or bed and get outside or in the gym. The bodies' naturally produced endorphins will override and reduce stress, anxiety and toxicity.

Efficient transportation systems that integrate (rather) than isolate communities and their residents are critical. It can be as simple as connecting existing bike paths or sidewalks through design and integration to link with rail or roadways.

The average commute time has increased. Many commuters entering New York, New York, San Francisco, California and Los Angeles, California now can spend up to three to six hours of their day traveling into their places of work. This is not efficient. Density is critical to urban centers. It is unavoidable. The public and employees should not have to increase their risk of heart disease and other sedentary related health issues.

The United States has become a nation of morbidly obese people. They must have the opportunity to purchase affordable high-rise housing, which would enable urban residents to walk to work instead of driving.

It is tragic that the myth of automobile usage conveyed in television advertising is one of an automobile flying along an empty road with fit occupants. Nothing could be further from the truth; most people when they step out of their cars are still morbidly over-weight.

It doesn't have to be this way.

Matthew Myers surveying the slope in California for riding and jumping.

Outside experiencing the National Park Service (NPS) and California
Park systems infrastructure.

Investment in park systems is an investment in America's future. It stimulates new growth through tourism and its surrounding economic activity. It is the ultimate multiplier effect in economics. Millions of people travel to California and the west to experience the scenic beauty of the state and neighboring locations throughout the mid-west. They spend money in hotels, on gas, food and other items. Modern park systems have constructed amazing trail systems and integrated hiking, running, cycling and other activities creating venues for physical fitness.

When I was riding with my good friends, my brother and other teammates (pictured above), my brain was stimulated. In the action and flow of the moment new ideas for work and the technology that I have been developing emerged. But the activities impact was even greater than this: Concepts and projects that I had not anticipated emerged.

Infrastructure is critical for a highly innovative and healthy society.

Matthew featured in a remote location.

Energy Analysis and Reducing U.S. Government's Dependence on Fossil Fuels (Decreasing its Strategic Vulnerability)

Overview of Strategic Management Issues Required

Strategic Management involves managerial decisions that determine the long-run performance of the U.S. government and its overall economy's reliance on foreign oil[4]. Strategic management emphasizes the reviewing of internal and external opportunities and risks in strengths, weaknesses, opportunities and threats via (SWOT) analysis.[5]

The U.S. Department of Energy (DOE), the U.S Department of Transportation (DOT) and the United States Armed Forces through a cooperative initiative in partnership with the private sector must review all of their options and develop an overarching plan and framework to begin to shift the U.S. economy and military away from overdependence on fossil fuels.

---

[4]Thomas L. Wheelen and J. David Hunger. Strategic Management and Business Policy. Pearson Prentice Hall. 2008.
[5]*Id.*

It is also likely to require the direct involvement of the U.S. oil industry as they stand to be significantly impacted by a transition from fossil fuel in order to be effective. It will probably require that the oil industry be a direct recipient of profits from new energy sources through a diversification of their portfolio of products and services.

Instability in the U.S. Government's Over-Reliance on Foreign Fossil Fuels and the Long Term Strategic Management of These Risks

What will the collective strategy of the U.S government's (DOE, DOT and the collective U.S. Armed Forces) response be to offset the military and U.S. economies dependence on foreign oil and fossil fuels as a major driving force of the economy? How will the Armed Forces fuel their warships, planes and tanks to defend the country in a time of crisis or attack if world supplies are restricted by OPEC and other oil producing nations? How can the U.S. government realistically begin the process of becoming less dependent on foreign fossil fuels?

What funding initiatives can the U.S. government take to fund or sponsor initiatives to create hydroelectric, fuel cell, solar or a new yet-to-be determined energy source to power the nation's economic development and national defense needs?

How will the U.S. realistically fund a non-fossil fuel initiative in addition to the costs of the current conflict in Iraq and Afghanistan, loans to large financial institutions to prevent their bankruptcy and loans to the U.S. auto industry to keep them solvent?

These are questions that have remained largely unaddressed over a ten (10) year period from 2007 to 2017. They are questions that should continue to be at the forefront of economic and policy discussions.

Shift from U.S. Dependence on Foreign Fossil Fuels

Coal and Natural Gas Consumption in 2008

A DOE Energy Information Administration (EIA) Brochure *Greenhouse Gases, Climate Change & Energy* notes that the "U.S. economy is the largest in the world and it meets 85 percent of its energy needs through burning fossil fuels."[6]

This same brochure notes that petroleum accounted for 40% of U.S. primary energy consumption, with coal making up 23%, natural gas 22% and non-fossil 15%.[7] The 40% number was significant because a large percentage of the oil is imported from sources outside of the U.S.

The U.S. according to an EIA fact sheet *U.S. Coal Supply and Demand* notes that in 2007 exports of coal exceeded imports.

---

[6]*Greenhouse Gases, Climate Change & Energy. Energy Information Institute*. Department of Energy. DOE/EIA-X012. May 2008. http://www.eia.doe.gov/bookshelf/brochures/greenhouse/Chapter1.htm.
[7]*Id.*

Exports were 59.2 million short tons and imports were 36.3 million short tons for a net export total of 22.8 million short tons.[8] Overall coal production in 2007 totaled 1,145.6 million short tons.[9] This is a noteworthy figure because it means that the U.S. isn't a major importer or exporter of coal.

It has substantial reserves of coal. Imported natural gas "represents almost 18 percent of the gas consumed in the United States annually, compared with 11 percent just 12 years ago."[10] Natural gas consumption after 2008 began to increase considerably in the U.S., and coal usage began to decline.

---

[8]Fred Freme. *U.S. Coal Supply and Demand: 2007 Review.* Energy Information Institute. Energy Information Administration. Data for 2007. Report Released: April 2008.

[9]*Id.*

[10]*About U.S. Natural Gas Pipelines – Transporting Natural Gas.* Fact Sheet. Energy Information Administration. Official Energy Statistics from the U.S. Government. 2007.
http://www.eia.doe.gov/pub/oil_gas/natural_gas/analysis_publications/ngpipeline/impex.html.

Coal, and Natural Gas Consumption in 2016

In 2016, coal consumption shifted to approximately 30.4%[11] of U.S electricity generation. This represented a slight decrease in usage, attributed in part to the rise of low cost natural gas, which now accounts for 33.8% of U.S. energy consumption for electricity.[12] It is worth noting that coal, despite the media's recent discussion of the U.S. coals industry decline still represented nearly 30% of the U.S. energy consumption for electricity generation.

In 2016, natural gas consumption had increased to approximately "29% of total U.S. primary energy consumption in 2016."[13] This remarkable growth in natural gas represented a nearly 60% increase (from 18% to 29%) over a nearly 10 year period. This increase should be expected to rise.

---

[11]*Frequently Asked Questions: What is U.S. electricity generation by energy source?* U.S. Energy Information Administration. 2016.
[12]*Id.*
[13]*Frequently Asked Questions, How much natural gas is consumed in the United States?* U.S. Energy Information Administration. 2016.

Natural gas is a cleaner fuel source (from an emissions perspective) and has newer infrastructure and distribution channels in place to support the marketplace. The supply chain has been modernized, with aggressive fracking of shale and other oil exploration activities.

U.S. Military's Reliance on Foreign Imports

2008 Analysis

The U.S. Energy Information Administration (EIA) in their July 2008 *Crude Oil and Total Petroleum Imports Top 15 Countries* noted that the U.S. is heavily dependent on imports from Canada, Mexico, the Middle East, South America and Russia. The EIA report found that the "top ten sources accounted for approximately 87 percent of all U.S. crude oil imports."[14] This means that the U.S. (according to these figures) the U.S. is only able to produce 13% of its oil needs for 40% of its energy requirements.

---

[14]*Crude Oil and Total Petroleum Imports Top 15 Countries.* Fact Sheet. Energy Information Administration: Official Energy Statistics from the U.S. Government. September 15, 2008.
http://www.eia.doe.gov/pub/oil_gas/petroleum/data_publications/company_level_imports/current/import.html.

With the rise of natural gas nearly ten (10) years later the United States has become more capable of producing energy conservation measures and a shift from primary dependence on fossil fuels through a substantial investment and partnership with the private sector to develop other fuel sources. Existing domestic coal reserves can be used (as measures by the DOE and DOT) to ensure that the U.S. Armed Forces have sufficient reserves to support their infrastructure and national defense. A Wednesday, June 4, 2008 article entitled *250,000 top-off* notes that the U.S.S. Lake Erie required a 250,000-gallon top off at sea "ahead of an anti-ballistic-missile test".[15] This was more than $1/3^{rd}$ of the ship's 600,000-gallon capacity.[16] In 2008 White House economic advisor Edward Lazear noted that "the recent spike in oil prices, if sustained, could shave as much as 1.5 percentage points off of U.S. economic growth this year."[17]

---

[15]Gregg K. *Kakesako. 250,000 top-off.* The Star Bulletin. Vol 13, Issue 156. Wednesday, June 4, 2008.

[16]*Id.*

[17]James Dalgleish. *Oil price spike could shave off GDP growth: White House.* Thomson Reuters. 2008.http://www.reuters.com/article/newsOne/idUSWAT00956720080528

2017 Analysis

The more recent fall in prices in 2017[18] should not be a deterrent to shifting the strategic focus away from oil or building the necessary infrastructure to support this. The price of a barrel on November 10, 2017 is approximately $56.74.[19] This price can be expected to rise or fall significantly based on market supply and geopolitical activity. Pursuant to the U.S. Energy Information "In 2016, U.S. net imports (imports minus exports) of petroleum from foreign countries were equal to about 25% of U.S. petroleum consumption."[20] Further reducing the country's dependence on foreign oil sources can only further benefit the industries and corporations that rely on this infrastructure to support their operations.

---

[18]Stephanie Landsman. CNBC. April 7, 2017.
http://www.cnbc.com/2017/04/07/how-soaring-oil-prices-could-cost-you-at-the-gas-pump-rbc-says.html.
[19]NASDAQ. November 11, 2017.
http://www.nasdaq.com/markets/crude-oil.aspx
[20]*Frequently Aced Questions. How much oil consumed by the United States comes from foreign countries?* U.S. Energy Information Institute. 2016.

Why Are Energy Sources for Electricity Generation So Important?

Regardless of cyclical price fluctuations in oil, or a rise in natural gas production and usage in the United States a shift away from a complete dependence on oil has incredible value. As a government and industry strategy a movement away from this dependence would lessen the impact of the U.S. on foreign oil reserves to power its transportation, economic and military needs.

Coal and natural gas reserves can be used to supplement the development of energy to power the U.S. particularly as new power sources are designed to offset the country's dependence on foreign oil. It is also strategically important for the U.S. to retain oil reserves for military, plastic and pharmaceutical production. The process should be considered a long-term strategy but it will require active participation and funding on the part of the U.S. government in cooperation with private sector industries.

Driving through parts of coal country in Virginia and Pennsylvania reveals communities that have drastically shifted as demand for coal has been offset by solar power and renewable energy. I have driven past boarded-up businesses that used to contain coffee shops, hardware stores, laundromats, bars, furniture stores, movie theaters and other merchants. Now these buildings are empty, a by-product of shifting industrial, commercial and residential energy demand, with turbines and solar panels that are manufactured at extremely low cost in China and other parts of the world.

Upstate Connecticut (throughout Winsted and Torrington) has been hit particularly hard by the shift in manufacturing to a service based economy. Entire sections of the downtown are empty, with buildings set for public auction, lease, and/or are going out of business. Auto repair, thrift stores and a few gas stores are the principle businesses that remain on the main-street in Winsted.

Winsted, Connecticut vacancies.

The same is true of Torrington, which has huge swaths of beautiful brick buildings, with their original windows, just waiting to re-purposed for a new technology headquarters; corporate manufacturing center; or even lofts and apartment housing. They can be renovated with the same attention to detail that an early 19th or 20th Century residential building can. The original structures have hardwood floors, steel pilings and other structural enhancements that make the buildings a sound investment.

Torrington, Connecticut vacant factories.

The renovations of these low cost buildings (due to abandonment or neglect) are examples of how the multiplier effect works in the surrounding communities. New and existing plumbing and electrical contactors move into the area to service the industry. Lunch wagons and restaurants and dry cleaners open in the proximity of the headquarters. New housing springs up around the new re-purposed corporate office. Existing housing is renovated. Each of these businesses from the largest to the smallest is a critical ingredient. These retrofits cause a gradual reversal of the decline of a community.

New U.S. Energy Initiative (2003 to 2017 Comparison)

Introduction

It is important for the U.S. federal government (particularly the DOE and DOT) to fund energy development programs that can be used to supplement new energy initiatives. The U.S. government should not have an immediate expectation of a rapid or immediate transition to economic development and military operations that are powered by other energy sources.

2008 National Defense Funding

The U.S government may also be limited in the amount of money that they can loan private sector industries to develop new power technologies, increase coal, natural gas production, electrical generation and generally develop factories and transportation systems that are less dependent on foreign oil.

The federal government may be constrained because of their recent loans to the financial services sector and the overall funding of the wars in Iraq and Afghanistan. An Associated Press article on September 19, 2008 notes that,

The federal government already has pledged more than $600 billion in the past year to bail out, or help bail out, some of the biggest names in American finance. That includes the rescue of investment bank Bear Stearns in March, the takeover of mortgage giants Fannie Mae and Freddie Mac earlier this month and the takeover of the world's largest insurance company, American International Group, just this week.[21]

This $600 billion is in addition to the nearly $850 billion that has been spent overseas in Iraq and Afghanistan.

A CBS News article notes that President George W. Bush's war funding measure "will bring the amount Congress has provided for the Iraq war since it began in 2003 to more than $650 billion. For war operations in Afghanistan, the measure will bring the total to nearly $200 billion congressional officials said."[22]

[21]Tom Raum and Jeanine Aversa, Associated Press Writers. Radical rescue: Hundreds of billions for bailout. The Associated Press. 2008. http://news.yahoo.com/s/ap/20080919/ap_on_bi_ge/financial_meltdown&.

[22]File from the Associated Press. *Bush signs $162B war spending bill for Iraq, Afghanistan*. CBS News. Monday, June 30, 2008. http://www.cbc.ca/world/story/2008/06/30/us-warfunding.html.

The total spending levels for these combined efforts are approximately $1.45 trillion dollars. The U.S. government has also provided the auto industry with $25 billion in loans for the conversion of its production line vehicles to more fuel-efficient models to date and they have requested $50 billion more to "help develop next generation fuel-efficient vehicles."[23]

---

[23]The Associated Press. *Auto industry seeks $50B in loans from Congress.* CNNMoney.com August 23, 2008.
http://money.cnn.com/2008/08/23/news/economy/auto_bailout.ap/index.htm.

As of October 24, 2017, the Congressional Budget Office estimates that the combined cost of the wars in Iraq and Afghanistan is estimated to be between $570 billion and $1.055 trillion between 2008 and 2017.[24]

Would this fiscal allocation be as high if the U.S. didn't need to defend its access to oil reserves in the Middle East? It is highly unlikely.

---

[24]State of Peter Orszag, Direct. Congressional Budget Office. CBO Testimony. E*stimated Costs of U.S. Operations in Iraq and Afghanistan and of Other Activities Related to the War on Terrorism.* October 24, 2017. https://www.cbo.gov/sites/default/files/110th-congress-2007-2008/reports/10-24-costofwar_testimony.pdf.

Can the United States benefit from a highly diversified energy strategy? Absolutely. Energy infrastructure investments are extremely valuable, providing long-term strategic cost savings and benefits. Energy infrastructure investments (with interest rates as low as they are in 2017) are a strategic investment for the future. In real 2017 dollars, even with the Federal Reserve raising rates a quarter point to 1.25%[25], they are still less expensive in 2017 dollars than they are in the future (inflation). In essence, it will cost more to invest in a high-speed rail in the future (cost of materials rises and purchasing power of dollar decreases), than it would if you invest in the project today.

---

[25]Jeff Cox. Fed hikes interest rates despite declining inflation, sets plan for balance sheet reduction. CNMC. June 14, 2017.

These substantial funding levels should not deter the U.S. government from making strategic investments in its own energy infrastructure and transportation needs. Instead policy makers that are supporting DOE and DOT funding initiatives should be prepared to deal with certain fiscal realities (which will limit the immediate funding outlays) that power supply development initiatives receive. The U.S. government in exchange for loans to the auto industry should have also created more significant milestones and other contractual requirements to make the transition to more fuel-efficient and non-fossil fuel based power supplies a long-term reality and not another temporary corrective measure. The oil industry must also be an active partner in the process and a key developer of new technologies otherwise the effort will be stalled by their intervention.

There is still an opportunity to develop fuel efficiency and alternative sources of power for the transportation industry, at the domestic individual user level (cars and trucks) and industry (trucking, rail and airlines).

Specific management guidelines will be required to successfully begin to transition the U.S. economy from a foreign fossil fuel driven economy and military to an economy balanced with natural gas, limited coal and other supplemental energy sources (wave, wind, solar and fuel-cell). Supplemental energy sources can include technologies that have been patented but shelved to develop until a later date.

Why is it so hard to implement renewable energy initiatives? Space and existing footprints. It is very difficult and expensive to retrofit existing facilities with new renewable energy technologies. A walk around the military bases in Hawai'i reveals limited space and aging facilities. Having personally led a team on a facilities condition assessment of Pearl Harbor it is clear that a complete retrofit of these operations would require a complete redesign of many structures. Many of the buildings have historical significance and are not able to accommodate solar panels or renovations. Others have classified manufacturing and services. Disrupting these functions could compromise national security.

When our team walked around the military base, we were met with resistance and uncertainty, despite our high level of clearance and critical natural of our work. Organizational culture and norms provide a significant roadblock and impediment to a successful renovation of a large and complex military base.

The other exceptionally large limitation is the extraordinary petroleum requirements to power the military's planes, tanks and ships. The military's operations require tens of millions of gallons of fossil fuel. Wind, solar and wave power can only power a fraction of the demands of the operations (the buildings, housings and command centers), until the ships, planes and tanks are actually redesigned to work with electric battery powered motors, fuel cells and other alternative sources of power.

Existing New Power Supply Sources

Analysis of 2008 New Power Supply Sources

The U.S. Government can focus on new initiatives that the American Wind Energy Association (AWEA) is sponsoring. The AWEA announced on September 3, 2008 that the "U.S. has installed over 20,000 MW of wind capacity, and is now the world leader in wind electricity generation with enough to power 5.3 million American homes."[26] Increasing installation of wind farms has the potential to power not only residential installations. They could also be used on military bases with adequate acreage to power residential and other operations in a limited fashion. Commercial operations could also supplement their operations with wind energy as applicable.

---

[26]Katie Fehrenbacher. U.S. Now the World Leader in Wind Electricity Generation. Earth2tech.com. September 3, 2008. http://earth2tech.com/2008/09/03/us-now-the-world-leader-in-wind-electricity-generation/.

Wind technology has expanded across the United States geographic footprint and has the potential to expand even further. The photo from the Tracy/Dublin region in Northern California illustrates wind technology that has been installed in close proximity to the existing utility grid.

When I have driven past wind farm installations one of the most striking things that stands out from direct observation is the maintenance schedule. In many cases the turbines that are no longer operating (rotating) are left inoperable. This is due in part to the cost of reinstallation, parts and labor. However, the infrastructure is in place. As the cost of the turbines falls, this will incentivize wind power conglomerates to replace worn out turbines and generators.

Another major issue is the complexity of storage and transmission. Many of the wind turbines that I have ridden past in Hawai'i, California, Oklahoma and Connecticut are in close proximity to the existing power grid. What is less apparent (on closer visual inspection) to the casual observer is the lack of battery systems to store the power. If wind power is to expand to include a greater percentage of U.S power the issue of battery systems needs to be resolved.

Wind turbines near Tracy, California.

Wind energy, according to the U.S. Energy Information Institute now accounts for nearly 8% of U.S. energy production.[27]

---

[27]Wind and solar in March accounted for 10% of U.S. electricity generation for first time. Energy Information Institute. June 14, 2017. https://www.eia.gov/todayinenergy/detail.php?id=31632.

Geothermal energy is an excellent source of heating energy, requiring significant upfront excavation costs. However, the ability to harness the power of the earth's heat is exceptional. The image below shows volcanic activity. Harnessing the heat of an active volcano is not possible at this point in time. Capturing radiant heat from beneath the earth's surface is a viable option and has been done in locations like Hawai'i, including the Big Island.

I woke up one morning at 3:00 a.m. and hiked out on to an active lava flow with a colleague. The power of the earth's core is extraordinary. The heat even in the early hours of the morning is exceptional. Harnessing this heat to generate steam and power turbines sounds outlandish, but it is actually a very viable option for generating power. The turbines can't be located in an unstable location that is subject to collapse at any moment like this volcano. But they serve as an example of what is possible with power that is a fundamental aspect of the earth's core.

The temperature on the surface of an active lava field can reach up to 160°F and the vapor from the lava hitting the ocean water creates steam that is scalding. Designing infrastructure to capture volcanic energy and generate steam to power turbines is costly, complex and very risky, both to human life and equipment operability. However, geothermal energy has been demonstrated to be a viable power source and should continue to be explored.

Matthew Myers examining the active lava flow entering the ocean. Disclaimer – Helicopter approach to an active lava flow is advisable.

Included is a photo from a hike out to an active lava (directly over the crust) flow (in an undisclosed location).

Bankruptcy of Emerging Technology Providers – Hawai'ian Example – HOKU®

Hawaii's own energy providers including Hoku® (Nasdaq: HOKU) which has chosen to locate its solar module and polysilicon manufacturing in Idaho because of significantly "better tax incentives, lower electricity costs, money for infrastructure improvements and state grants to train new employees"[28] can also be viewed as an expanding new power supplier. The U.S. government/private sector partnership can accomplish their strategic energy supply shift by engaging in a partnership with industry that fully utilizes the phases of strategic management.[29]

Despite the natural abundance of sunlight in Hawai'i and the company's expansion to the U.S. mainland, HOKU® eventually declared bankruptcy and was acquired by a Chinese conglomerate.

However, early adopters in a highly competitive marketplace are not always the last standing. They are instrumental in driving the cost of the technology down.

---

[28]Pacific Business News Staff. *Hoku chooses Idaho for solar business.* Pacific Business News. Wednesday, August 30, 2006.
[29]*Id.*, refer to Footnote 1.

2017 Analysis of Corporate Interest in Solar, Wind and its Related Ecosystem

Tesla® has moved aggressively into the solar marketplace. More recently Tesla® acquired Solar City®[30] after the company was hit hard by the proliferation of low cost Chinese panels and a highly competitive U.S. marketplace.

Tesla® most recently announced rooftop panels that are shaped like architect's grade fiberglass and asphalt composite shingles would be introduced. It is unclear at this point in time if the market (at-large) will adopt these innovative products.

The potential is huge: Making a solar panel aesthetically pleasing and design based, like Apple® and Tesla® cars shifts the product away from being purely utilitarian and couples it with a holistic vision of a house or building that powers their product (car and appliances).

---

[30]Mike Ramsey and Cassandra Sweet. Tesla and Solar City Agree to $2.6 Billion Deal. August 1, 2016.
https://www.wsj.com/articles/tesla-and-solarcity-agree-to-2-6-billion-merger-deal-1470050724.

Limiting this vision to consumers only is myopic and fails to understand the broader market potential. Industry and military can use this type of technology and infrastructure to power their fleets, with the additional incentive of providing parking armatures for sunlight coverage.

The critical challenge to the electric car industry is the charge station infrastructure, which has limited distribution and coverage, like access to diesel for engines designed to use this fuel. This is a critical issue for the expansion of the industry.

The American Wind Energy Association (AWEA) representation of the wind generation industry, Solar City® and other energy providers in the U.S. present the opportunity for a complete shift in how transportation and manufacturing systems and military operations conduct business. These new industries have the potential to change how energy is produced and distributed in the U.S.; and how it is used to supplement new and emerging industries and the military with a non-fossil fuel based power supply. A great deal of opportunity and risk exists with this strategic management initiative which requires strengths, weaknesses, opportunities and threats (SWOT) analysis of the United States dependence on foreign oil.[31]

Later entrants like Solar City® (and like HOKU® before them) will also struggle with a marketplace that becomes more and more flooded with inexpensive panels and innovative technologies (that are able to compete with their roofing singles) with the massive oil energy infrastructure that remains well capitalized and globally dominates.

---

[31] *Id.*

It is critical to note that the solar power for electricity generation only represents 2.0% of U.S. energy production (and wind is only slightly more significant at 8.0%).[32] This is up from 0.9% of U.S. energy production (and wind is only slightly more significant at 5.6%) in 2016. Solar needs to move more into the range of 10 to 15% of U.S. energy production (and wind to within the same percentage range) in order to be truly substantive and represent a significant percentage of U.S. electricity generation. It is possible to increase this percentage (wind, solar, et. al.) from approximately 15% to 30% over the next decade.

The United States should encourage U.S. manufacturing in this area – creating jobs and industry to power its own enterprises. As the cost of these technologies continues to fall, market adoption will follow. However, the alternative energy industry can continue to expect bankruptcies from the wind, solar and other renewables categories. Separately, natural gas (a cleaner) oil product can be expected to increase its market share of U.S. energy production.

---

[32] *Wind and solar in March accounted for 10% of U.S. electricity generation for first time.* Energy Information Institute. June 14, 2017. https://www.eia.gov/todayinenergy/detail.php?id=31632.

Wave and water energy (dams and turbidity turbines) have the potential to harness the extraordinary power of water of providing energy to millions of homes, businesses and industries. Dams already serve this function. The Hoover Dam, which was completed in 1936, provides electricity to the region. The Bonneville Dam in Oregon (shown below) is another example of hydroelectric power generating 1,218 MW of power of an annual basis.[33] Transmission lines and distribution systems are the critical component of any major power provider.

Photo credit: Stephen S. Myers. Bonneville Dam, Oregon.

---

[33]Bonneville Lock and Dam. 2017.
http://www.nwp.usace.army.mil/bonneville/.

Having visited the west, including many hydroelectric and dam projects, it is easy to underestimate the time and resources that were required to build facilities like Lake Mead in Nevada, or the Hoover Dam. They have significant costs and benefits, as do any large infrastructure projects, disrupting the natural flow of watersheds, but providing (in some cases) a large cycling path around the dam.

I was able to cycle around Lake Mead with a friend from Las Vegas. The recreation area that has been constructed in and around the dam is peaceful, restorative and provides miles of cycling and running opportunities.

Cycling crew for Lake Mead, Nevada and other California locations.

Photo credit: Stephen S. Myers. Bonneville Dam, Oregon transmission lines.

Ocean power doesn't have significant examples of deployment in the U.S. It has the potential to be a significant percentage of U.S. energy production, but has largely been limited to research and military applications to date. Ocean energy production, although it has the least practical working applications, has the greatest potential. It is capital intensive, requiring expensive precision turbines, capable of withstanding hurricane force, but is a limitless source of energy.

Imagine a high-speed rail running from New York to Los Angeles, Los Angeles to San Francisco, and New York to Miami, San Francisco to Seattle, Seattle to Chicago, Chicago to Boston and Boston to New York, all powered by wave energy and corresponding transmission and battery retention systems.

Battery Systems

Tesla® has partnered with French energy company Noeon® to build a 100MW/129MWh battery connected a wind farm in Australia.[34] The primary issue with battery technology is access to rare earth metals. The marketplace for rare metals is dominated by China. Developing other types of metal and non-metal battery systems should be the primary goal of government and corporate research and development (R&D) in the United States.

Wind, wave and solar power that are connected to battery systems have the potential to power large residential, corporate and industrial operations. At the residential level Tesla® also has the Powerwall™ battery system, which has 14 kWh of capacity and costs approximately $6,200, not including installation.[35]

---

[34]Sarah Kimmorley, Paul Cogan, Business Insider Australia. Tesla is going to build the world's largest lithium ion battery in Australia. July 6, 2017. http://www.businessinsider.com/tesla-to-build-worlds-largest-lithium-ion-battery-in-australia-2017-7
[35]Tesla. *Powerwall.* 2017. https://www.tesla.com/powerwall.

The system combined with Tesla's® solar rooftop technology has the potential to power the Tesla® cars and portions of the house itself. One issue is access to rare metals[36]; and the heavy cost of extraction and reclamation of these metals. Another issue is the shift in the amortization and payback period associated with adding battery systems to financing options for solar technology resulting in a longer timeframe.

[36]The Electric Car Revolution Is Making These Investors Very Optimistic. Reuters. October 5, 2016.
http://fortune.com/2016/10/05/electric-car-revolution-investors-lithium-rare-earth-metals/.

Examination of the Payback Period from a Rooftop Solar Installation

The purpose of this analysis[37] is to propose a business implementation plan that will enable a Hawai'i medical (herein HMJV) business to meet the numerous challenges it faces in Hawaii's current economic climate. By pursuing the initiative presented in this implementation plan, HMJV will be able to achieve all three of its major goals: 1) improve the patient experience, 2) improve the employee experience, and 3) improve the profitability of HMJV.

Today, HMJV is the largest dental group practice in the State of Hawaii with ten locations throughout the islands, including: four locations on Oahu, three on the Big Island, two on Maui and one on Kauai. Since 1986, HMJV has served nearly 100,000 patients.

---

[37]Due to an NDA with Infrastructure Upgrade, Inc. the name of the business proposing the commercial solar installation is withheld.

Under its current management the company has grown into a profitable company with Earnings before Interest, Taxes, Depreciation and Expenses (EBITDA) of approximately eight percent (8%). The company's occupancy costs (rent and utilities) are currently approximately $2.2 million or ten percent (10%) and HMJV is seeking to reduce these costs and increase EBITDA in 2018.

A team from Infrastructure Upgrade, Inc.® has been asked to develop a plan to help reduce occupancy costs in order to make HMJV more profitable. Creating a sustainable profitable business model is an additional goal that the team intends to strive for and present in the attached plan.

Infrastructure Upgrade, Inc.® recommends HMJV reduce its overhead costs and increase its EBITDA through photovoltaic (PV) projects on their medical centers throughout the state of Hawaii.

As a pilot program HMJV is proposing to install a photovoltaic system on the roof of their Kauai business located in a commercial office space on Lihue, Kauai. This initial project, if successful, would be expanded to Oʻahu and other HMJV medical centers across the state. The initial project would require the formation of a separate business entity (SBE) entitled "HMJV, LLC." In time, the LLC hopes to service additional clientele throughout the state of Hawaii with photovoltaic solutions.

Mission and Objectives

HMJV, LLC is a separate business entity owned and operated by HMJV. HMJVJV, LLC will execute "Option #2" outlined in the formal business plan. The installation of a PV parking-canopy system consists of a two-phase process. The first phase primarily focuses on the HMJV medical center by installing approximately 420 PV panels on a parking-canopy system on the east-facing parking lot. The second phase primarily focuses on the rest of the commercial property by installing approximately 1,000 PV panels on a parking-canopy system on the larger south-facing parking lot. The size, scale, and complexity of the PV system make it an intricate sustainable initiative.

This canopy would provide: (1) a framework for the solar panels needed to generate electricity; and (2) covered parking for all tenants and customers visiting the commercial property. Electricity from the panels will be sold by HMJV, LLC to HMJV and other Commercial property tenants and the excess electricity sold to Kauai Island Utility Cooperative (KIUC). HMJV and Commercial property tenants will purchase electricity at a discounted rate and KIUC will purchase electricity based on a Schedule "Q" Tariff negotiated agreement. This agreement is federally mandated and the rate is a derivative of KIUC's base costs.

By installing PV power at its Kauai medical center HMJV will increase its triple bottom line (profit, planet, people) by decreasing its utility expenses and increasing its revenue. Additionally, HMJV will become an eco-efficient business helping the environment and setting an ethical business example in Hawaii.

Through HMJV we believe that HMJV can also take advantage of state and federal tax credits (but not the State of Hawaii's Act 221-Qualified High Tech Business (QHTB) 100% tax credit), which will further improve HMJV's profitability. HMJV can install the solar panels with an estimated payback period of less than two years and receive great public relations and marketing opportunities. It can also increase the retention of its employees by promoting a sustainable environment, recruiting top caliber talent who are interested in living "green" and increasing the productivity of its employees.

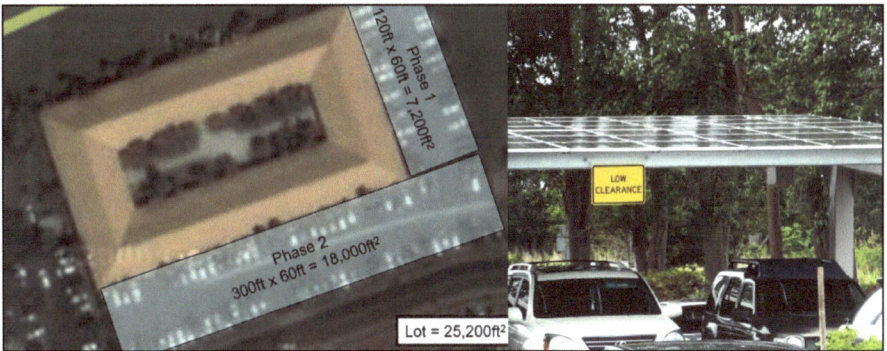

Parking canopy for proposed photovoltaic installation on Lihue, Kauai'i.

A solar energy covered parking structure is an easy addressable solution, having visited several active facilities in Hawai'i and North Carolina. It is great to be able to pull under a solar armature. When I have returned to my vehicle after a site visit, it is a pleasure to open a cool shaded car.

It provides an easy renewable energy fix. Millions of square feet of parking lots exist in the United States and the world, representing a huge market opportunity for design and installation.

Project Opportunities

HMJV, LLC has three main project opportunities:

1.) Reduce HMJV Utility Costs;

2.) Create a new diversified profit center;

3.) Be pro-active environmental leaders throughout the state of Hawaii.

These three opportunities could have profound effects on the profitability of HMJV. The opportunity to diversify HMJV's family of companies with a non-dental related entity could mitigate future risks associated with a slump in the dental industry. This could protect the company from future hardship and provide an additional profit center or expansion opportunity. HMJV, LLC also offers a new environmental leadership role for the HMJV owners and operators. This environmental leadership role could increase HMJV employee productivity while also increasing revenue due to consumer support of this new initiative.

Business Model

The proposed commercial property project Option #2 is a sound business model. This model requires the introduction of a new separate business entity HMJV, LLC on Kauai. It also involves a review of the pro forma financial estimates that were constructed based on the current power consumption at the commercial property building on Kauai; and the amount of available space needed to install a comprehensive PV system. The estimated cost to execute Option #2 is $1.7 million. This capital investment expenditure will *not* be offset by federal and state tax credits as Act 221, Qualified High Tech Business – QHTB was phased out in 2011. This QHTB tax credit would have provided a one hundred (100%) return to any investor through a tax credit payback period of five years. Instead the payback period increases to approximately 6.5 years without QHTB credits

However, HMJV, LLC also has the opportunity to capitalize on a thirty percent (30%) Federal Tax credit and thirty-five percent (35%) state tax credit. This strategic approach of capitalizing on tax credits help prioritize HMJV, LLC & HMJV's capital expenditures while providing a safe return on investment. The tax credits will also help entice outside investment by improving payback periods although these tax credits are not totally essential in order for the commercial property project to be financially feasible.

HMJV also intends to generate estimated revenue of $94,119.00 per year by executing this PV solution on the commercial property. Revenue will be generated through the sale of electricity. Electricity will be sold to HMJV and Commercial property tenants at a rate of $0.30 per KWHr.

This provides a cost savings to all of these tenants whom currently pay KIUC on average $0.39 per KWHr. The remaining excess electricity will be sold to KIUC at a "Schedule Q" rate of $0.125 per KWHr. Below is the payback period and IRR of option #2 with and without QHTB tax incentives.

Analysis: Option #2	With QHTB[38]		Without QHTB
Payback	0.80	< 5 years	1.66
Net Present Value (NPV)	$1,473,694.37	Positive	$818,456.07
Profitability Index (PI)	4.96	> 1	2.91
Internal Rate of Return (IRR)	118.69%	> WACC	51.18%
Modified Internal Rate of Return (MIRR)	14.99%	> WACC	12.51%
Equivalent Annual Annuity (EAA)	$150,099.03		$83,361.56

---

[38]Most Hawai'i QHTB subsidies, including Act 221, have been phased out due to pressure from the Hawai'ian electric and other utilities.

In addition to the revenue received by HMJV, LLC, HMJV will gain added benefit and added revenue for their participation and ownership of this sustainable initiative. The mission of HMJV will be greatly enhanced by being able to provide customers with health care services generated by solar power. This is a distinguishing feature that few other medical providers can claim. The company will be known as a provider that delivers its services with solar power generated on site. The added benefit of this initiative and HMJV being a leader in the "green movement" will modify the client mix. This change will help decrease cancellations and increase new patient appointments. Customers and employees will appreciate the covered parking and feel good about HMJV's new sustainable direction. Customers will also respect HMJV's position and be more appreciative of their services.

The combination of these two benefits will potentially equate to one new customer or one less cancelled appointment per day, which equals $400.00 of additional revenue per day. Over the course of the year this will equate to $100,000.00 of additional revenue for the HMJV Lihue clinic. HMJV will also receive a cost savings on electricity due to the lower rate charged by HMJV, LLC. This cost savings equals $7,500.00 per year. These two combined savings equals $107,500.00 per year for HMJV's Lihue Clinic and will propel their EBITDA from eight percent (8%) to thirteen point seven percent (13.7%).

The management team has determined that HMJV, LLC has a profitable business platform that will generate revenue of over $97,000.00 per year while also helping HMJV achieve an EBITDA of over thirteen percent (13%) per year. The benefits of executing a photovoltaic project at the commercial property can be realized by HMJV, HMJV, LLC and any outside investors whom invest in the project. The community of Kauai and the State of Hawai'i will also benefit by this additional sustainable movement.

Nuclear Power – Bankruptcy and Disaster - No Longer A Viable Option for U.S. (or Global Energy Production)

The extraordinary storage costs of spent reactor fuel[39] and safety issues (spent fuel proliferation to rouge nations, Fukushima, et. al.) associated with nuclear power *do not* make it a viable option for U.S. power production. The estimated cost of Yucca Mountain's decommissioning in 2133 is $96.2 billion in 2007 dollars.[40] Nuclear power will continue to be phased out (decommissioned) because the cost of building new power plants is cost prohibitive from a cost-benefit perspective. Westinghouse Electric Co.®, a unit of Toshiba Corp® filed for bankruptcy "hit by billions of dollars of cost overruns at four nuclear reactors under construction in the U.S. Southeast"[41]

---

[39]Yucca Mountain cost estimate rises to $96 billion. World Nuclear Association. 2017. Citing U.S. Department of Energy Estimates.
http://www.world-nuclear-news.org/WR-Yucca_Mountain_cost_estimate_rises_to_96_billion_dollars-0608085.html.
[40]*Id.*
[41]Tom Hals, Makikio Yamazaki and Tim Kelly. *Huge nuclear cost overruns push Toshiba's Westinghouse into bankruptcy.* Reuters. March 30, 2017.
http://www.reuters.com/article/us-toshiba-accounting-board-idUSKBN17006K.

The cost of the South Carolina project is $22 billion and the cost of the Georgia plant is $19 billion, with $8.3 billion in U.S. government loan guarantees.[42] The cost per kw/h is too high when factoring in construction, maintenance and long-term storage. Nuclear power is *not a viable option* for U.S. (or world power production) and should be completely phased out as soon as possible.

Shift to Natural Gas - Solar and Renewables from Nuclear

Will other utilities follow the path of other large utilities shifting their emphasis from nuclear to renewable energy adoption for its shareholders and venture funds?

Will other utilities follow this strategy nationwide?

At Infrastructure Upgrade, Inc.® we think so. The U.S government data from the U.S. Energy Information Administration (EIA) supports a shift into renewables and natural gas from other sources.

---

[42]*Id.*

Moving an Entire Military Base and Operation

In my own experience involving setting up the basing initiative to move the Marine Corps from Okinawa to Guam, the complexities of the U.S. military's operations are vast. Planning to move 18,000 troops and their dependents from one island to another is a challenging task. The power that it takes to operate the military's operations in terms of fuel and electricity is exceptional. Moving an entire base involves an extraordinarily complicated planning process. It is an exceptionally taxing proposition for the military, their spouses and family. It is a group that is already heavily impacted by frequent relocations. The stress and uncertainty of an additional transfer and deployment is magnified across 18,000 troops and their dependents, in addition to the massive civilian staff group that supports non-classified daily operations.

I sat down with the team in a secure location on Pearl Harbor, O'ahu with senior commanding officers, a general, our private sector joint venture (JV) team. I directly oversaw the cost analysis spreadsheets for each of the major studies, including aircraft carrier berthing and mooring capacity, roads, bridges, major utilities, housing, water, waste water and major auxiliary studies using my laptop. We completed all vendor negotiations from a central conference center. Site visits to remote locations were fulfilled to ensure the major studies were finalized.

Private industry and consulting groups formed the major support roles for each of the Task Orders. Particularly striking about the process is how fragmented the military's operations actually are and the high level of resources needed to align these fragmented pieces. On the surface the four branches of the U.S. military appear seamless. The funding and planning needed to tie them together quickly rises to tens of millions.

Analysis of the U.S. Economics Over Dependence on Foreign Fossil Fuels

A SWOT analysis must be conducted not only for potential new manufacturing entrants, but also for existing coal and natural gas providers, the oil industry and other private sector participants and the principle government agencies involved (DOE, DOT and Armed Forces). The SWOT review must be revised and updated frequently. Included below are some but not all of the elements of a SWOT analysis of the U.S. economy and its reliance on foreign oil.

One of oil's strengths is that it has been a relatively efficient and inexpensive fuel supply up until recently. It has also generally also been a stable source of fuel from a scarcity and availability perspective.

There are up to ten (10) significant oil suppliers to the U.S. which indicates that there are some importing alternatives, a strength against the country's complete dependence on domestic oil.[43]

---

[43]*Id.*

The U.S. economy's dependence on foreign oil has multiple weaknesses including, but not limited to, instability of certain key suppliers like Iraq and Venezuela. The Strategic Studies Institute of the U.S. Army War College has produced a text entitled *Promoting Stability and Security in Venezuela*[44] with the recognition that this country has significant political and economic issues to overcome.

---

[44]Jeffrey K. Wilson. *Promoting Stability and Security in Venezuela.* Strategic Studies Institute of the U.S. Army War College. Graduating Class of 1995.
http://www.strategicstudiesinstitute.army.mil/pubs/display-papers.cfm?q=33.

Venezuela and Iraq are included in the list of the top 10 sources for U.S. imports of oil.[45] Rising oil costs have also appeared to contribute to significant reductions in overall GDP growth.[46] The U.S. military itself is heavily reliant on imported oil to power its infrastructure. This is of concern with the current conflict in Iraq because the country is a significant oil producer. If the U.S. becomes involved in countries like Iraq and Venezuela in an attempt to impose stability it risks damaging the very infrastructure that is the fuel supply for its existing (and potential military, in the case of Venezuela) operations there. The U.S. is also weakened as a country economically (production and transportation cost increases) by not having a portfolio of energy sources that they can turn to as an alternative when the cost of oil rises significantly.

---

[45]*Id.*, refer to Footnote 8.
[46]*Id.*, refer to Footnote 11.

A shift from dependence on foreign oil creates a tremendous opportunity for the government and private sector industries including the oil industry to create a profitable new system of manufacturing and transportation infrastructure powered in part by existing reserves of coal and natural gas and then supplemented over the long-term by an increasing use of new power sources. The U.S. wind farm industry's capability to power 5.3 million homes is evidence of an expanding industry that has a great potential for profitability and market share growth.

One of the principle threats of the U.S's dependence of foreign oil reserves, in addition to instability in key markets, is the potential for other nations to begin to develop new power sources prior to the United States. They will then be able to capture the market share that U.S. companies subsequently will lose by not moving quickly to develop these technologies. It would be a significant *opportunity cost* to allow a European Union or Chinese competitor to develop the technology and infrastructure capabilities first (particularly if they were generated as a part of the U.S. R&D efforts), and then sell them back to our country and its industries at a profit.

Budgets for the DOE, DOT and U.S. Armed Forces are prepared on an annual basis and frequently updated. Their budgets and funding levels are approved by Congress (House and Senate) and signed (as applicable) in funding authorizations approved by the U.S. President. Future trend forecasts for U.S. spending levels are prepared by a multitude of non-government organizations (NGOs) and the individual government agencies like the DOT, DOE and U.S. Armed Forces. A master plan that incorporates the 4 basic phases of strategic management: basic financial development, forecast-based projecting, externally oriented (strategic) input and essential management[47] in addition to input from NGO and individual agency forecast efforts must be developed for the establishment of supplemental energy sources and their facilities. They must also be augmented by the use of coal and natural gas reserves that are available within the U.S. and do not have to be imported like foreign oil supplies. The DOE, DOT and the U.S. Armed Forces should conduct financial planning efforts jointly. They need to also involve the private sector industries that have the capability of developing new energy sources.

---

[47]*Id.*

Master planning efforts have to include a one year projected budget (Phase 1) that includes infrastructure upgrades to assist manufacturing facilities, transportation infrastructure and systems that can utilize coal and natural gas and then transition to a larger percentage of non-fossil fuel energy. The U.S. government should not expect the use of oil to completely disappear.

In Phase 2 of strategic management, the forecast planning stage, the U.S. government/private sector consortium should create five to ten year plans with specific budgetary guidelines for supporting the attraction of manufacturing and transportation mechanisms that can utilize a combination of coal and natural gas produced energy and ultimately increased non-fossil energy sources. These budgetary outlines could include investments in rail system upgrades, research and development facilities to implement the development of new power sources, land and coastal area allocations for wind and hydroelectric infrastructure development and training to transition new employees to roll-out a new transportation and power supply industry.

Phase 3 of the U.S. government/private sector's initiative must involve direct intervention and active management of the process (i.e. externally oriented strategic planning[48]) and have the regulatory cooperation of the government and private sector unions to be adaptable and adjust their planning efforts to accommodate any new trends that emerge in power supply sources developed in the research and development facilities sponsored by this partnership. The combined government agencies can engage in creating a collective umbrella policy to achieve their mission.

---

[48]*Id.*

In Phase 4 of the government and private sector's strategic management[49] communication efforts need to be at the highest level to create national bi-partisan funding for the implementation of plans that are developed. Information must be transparent on spending levels and infrastructure improvements completed in real time and those improvements and budgetary allocations that are projected to be finalized in future years. It is critical that in order to create stakeholder buy-in key private sector industries constantly be briefed on the progress of the effort. All participants in the framework should consider the strategic management process to be dynamic and constantly changing. This includes all written materials, communications and projected and actual budgetary allocations to underwrite the plan.

---

[49]*Id.*

Renewable Energy Initiatives and Distributed Power Generation

New renewable energy initiatives developed in partnership with government and private developers that include *distributed power generation* agreements (generators from multiple smaller sources – wind, renewable energy, solar that range from 3 – 10,000 kW in size) can result in the following: (1) increasing the operational efficiency of the electricity grid by lessening the cost of transporting the electricity over long distances; and (2) reducing the amount of energy lost as electricity is transmitted over those distances. Here are some potential candidates for *distributed power generation*:

1. Solar.

2. Wind.

3. Biomass Plants.

4. Small-Scale Micro Turbines via Hydroelectric and Ocean
   generation.

5. Fuel cells.

6. Co-generation (steam).

7.   Landfill capture (methane conversion).

8.   Small-scale geothermal.

As the cost of manufacturing these technologies is reduced (i.e. via economies of scale) these technologies will begin to become more competitive with large-scale utilities that burn coal, fossil fuels (natural gas and oil), large-scale hydroelectric and nuclear. Nuclear generation is a relatively inexpensive power solution per kWh; *only* if the cost of transporting, storing and securing spent reactor fuel is *not* factored in. When these costs are actually factored into the cost per kWh the cost of nuclear power generation is drastically increased. There are also significant health, safety and security issues associated with both its generation and storage. Nuclear power is *not* a rationale or viable option for the future's energy production and should be eliminated.

IHS Markit Technology® (formerly Solarbuzz.com®) provides the following cost-benefit information (in the chart below) on the following technologies. It is important to note that these figures do not appear to incorporate federal and state subsidies, which significantly reduce the cost per kWh for these technologies (particularly photovoltaic and wind). These costs continue to fall and the cost per kilowatt-hour is reduced with each innovation in technology and supply chain efficiency.

Solar Energy (Photovoltaic)	1-100 kilowatts	$6-10,000 per kWp or 20-40 cents per kWh
Micro turbines	30-300 kilowatts	$1,000 to $1,500 per installed kWp or 10 to 15 cents per kWh
Fuel cells	1-200 kilowatts	$3-4,000 per kWp or 10-15 cents per kWh
Wind Turbines	10 kilowatt - 2 Megawatt	$1500-$3000 kWp 5-10 cents per kWh (lower numbers associated with larger Wind Farms).
Internal combustion engines	50 kilowatt to 5 Megawatt	$400-900 per kWp
Central Power Generation	500-3000 Megawatt	$500-1000 per kWp

Chart Source: HIS Markit Technology® (formerly Solarbuzz.com)®.

These types of energy solutions (solar, wind, biomass plants, etc.) can be incorporated into schools, private and public housing (including those for low- and moderate-income persons), military installations and other commercial and residential developments.

How can the integration of these technologies be paid for (if they aren't covered by private and/or public funds)?

One solution includes assessing user fees to pay for the installation of these technologies and their maintenance on a per usage basis. This would be similar to fees that condominium owners pay to own a property as a part of an association.

In a commercial or residential development users would pay for financing distributed power generation as a part of their monthly lease agreement. Similar strategies could be employed for paying to install innovative renewable energy and building technologies into low- and moderate-income housing, new housing developments, military bases and commercial high-rises. Other building design innovations (Energy Star® appliances, low-water usage water systems other installations or retrofits) could be paid for in this same manner.

There is significant remaining capacity for cogeneration. The Congressional Budget Office's (CBO) *Prospects for Distributed Electricity Generation* notes that "looking to the future, the EIA projects that additions of electricity generating capacity between 2000 and 2025 will total almost 450,000 megawatts."[50]

---

[50]Prospects for Distributed Electricity Generation. Congressional Budget Office (CBO). September 1, 2003.
https://www.cbo.gov/publication/14750.

For urban and rural buildings including housing, schools and other building projects, co-generation facilities can be integrated into the design of new projects and communities and/or the retrofit of existing ones.

Additionally, the report notes that "there are reasons to expect that distributed generation could meet a significant portion of future electricity demand in the United States, at costs that could compete with those of generation from new central power plants." The statement suggests that as the efficiency of manufacturing processes improves the overall cost of these technologies will be reduced. This claim is largely true, as the initial cost of manufacturing is very high and the early entrants into the marketplace pay substantial higher prices for cell phones, laptops, tablets, solar panels and other technologies.

Critical to rolling out new technologies are the exceptionally high costs of marketing the technologies to the public and industry through traditional print, television and now (in instances) social media.

In essence it is a basic tenant of economics that cost will be driven down by new manufacturing entrants (competitors) supplying a greater number of solar panels.

Financing for U.S. manufacturing of many renewable technologies has been limited, forcing U.S. installers of solar panels to purchase components from China, requiring complicated freight forwarding agreements, importing fees and other duties associated with bringing these products to the United States.

It is important that the U.S. *not* lose its competitive advantage or its opportunity to be a leader in distributed power generation by failing to have programs that support the underwriting, development and manufacturing of innovative renewable energy technologies in the U.S.

Housing and the Federal Umbrella (HUD)

Overview and Recommended Strategy

Federal, state and local guidelines for the development of low- and moderate-income housing are precise. They are spelled out with clarity. However the actual execution of the HUD and affordable housing guidelines (outlined below) is far from consistent. It is rarely even executed properly.

When I have walked through low- and moderate-income housing projects and homeless residential service providers in Hawai'i there have been significant hurdles for wheel chair accessibility, peeling lead paint, proper sewage hookups and damages to the flooring, walls and ceilings from water. The windward sides of all of the Hawai'ian islands, including O'ahu receive significant amounts of rain (during some storms – several inches per hour).

This is revealed in the poor quality of the housing and homeless services provided in these instances (mold from water damages creates respiratory problems for individuals living in these structures). New housing projects (before the opening ribbon has been cut) have shown sloppy installation, with hardware (hinges and door knobs, bathroom fixtures and sinks) that is loose or improperly installed.

Included is a low- and moderate-income site that my brother and I provided extensive repairs and clean-up for. It is typical of the incompetence and neglect that most families experience when dealing with affordable housing. The photos show a truckload of termite filled construction lumber that was left in the basement of the property after repairs were made.

The construction team left framing nails and asphalt in the gravel driveway as fill, creating a safety risk for tenants, including damage to their tires. The site was filled with poison ivy, hornets, broken glass and extensive overgrown weeds. Nearly seventy bags of yard debris and termite filled construction debris (framing lumber) were taken to the Buncombe County, North Carolina landfill for their green waste program. The composite photo that includes the white truck filled with lumber demonstrates evidence of this property's total neglect and gross negligence. Other images show the bagged trash (filled with broken glass, concrete, framing nails and debris). The windows sashes were filled with peeling window glaze, dry rot and lead paint (samples of the lead paint were taken as evidence). Many of the windows had broken glass, including the image of my hand being placed through the aluminum door for effect. The doors hinges were broken and included peeling paint. The sinks didn't drain properly and the kitchen cabinets were missing pull knobs and filled with trash. The washing machine was not properly hooked up, causing water to pour down from the 2nd story to the first story. Plugging vacuum cleaners in the site resulted in dangerous electrical shorting from many of the outlets. The photos below are typical and represent the majority of low- and moderate-income housing. Particularly problematic about this property was that its ownership was a church, with plenty of resources for deferred maintenance. In cases like this the proper local, state and Federal authorizes need to be notified, including law enforcement (due to significant safety issues and hazards).

Total property negligence documented at low- and moderate-income housing.

A comprehensive list of the recommended procurement, building and services strategies is included below. The twenty-four items provides an introduction and is by no means all-inclusive. Not-for-profits and corporations struggle or fail to meet most of the requirements outlined.

Subject projects selected as a part of municipalities housing procurement process need to engage in the following due diligence in order to be selected and complete their projects successfully:

1) Proper financial management (including strict adherence to financial audits and financial reporting requirements);

2) Adherence to applicable state and federal procurement laws;

3) Prohibition of ineligible project activities that may violate HUD rules and regulations (religious based activities, for-profit activities, etc.);

4) Adherence to applicable state and federal environmental laws, including lead based paint, hazardous material

remediation (as applicable) and guidance relating to noise and the storage of explosive/hazardous materials that are specific to HUD;

5) Adherence to state and federal labor standards;

6) Adherence to Section 103 regarding the employment of low- and very-low income persons;

7) Attempting to address long-term housing and community center needs by funding multi-year projects that adequately address the needs of low- and moderate-income persons and the homeless;

8) Developing projects that incorporate sustainability measures, including energy efficiency: solar – PV, solar water, wind; recycled materials; and other cost saving measures (thermal – coated panes, etc.);

9) Ensuring that the clientele are low- and moderate-income persons in either public service and/or construction, rehabilitation or renovation projects;

10) Complete disclosure of all tenants and activities in a proposed project in order make certain that the activities as a whole are eligible (for example, a facility that houses religious organizations, for-profit companies and Board Associations for private housing complexes);

11) Review of an organization's financial solvency and ability to manage federal funds;

12) Proper income, Social Security and W2 form disclosure of tenants and/or facilities to ensure their status as low- and moderate-income persons – active renewal and analysis of participants and/or tenants income status to ensure that they meet the criteria for eligibility;

13) Mandating that permits are in place to expedite any construction activities and that the applicant is aware of

HUD's Noise, Hazardous Materials and Runway Clear Zone requirements;

14) Ensuring that the proposed number of beneficiaries are actually served (i.e. if an applicant proposes to serve 100 persons that the agency has properly documented that 100 persons have been served, that they are the correct category of low- and moderate-income persons (elderly, children, homeless, etc.) and that beneficiaries have properly submitted their income documentation (as noted in item 12) if and where applicable;

15) It is important to note that the issues identified below need to be addressed when attempting to expedite the development of public housing in other states. Cross-checking the agency's business credentials in order to identify whether or not candidates for funding are registered to do business in the State of Hawaii (via Hawaii Compliance Express, the State Departments of Taxation, Labor and Commerce and Consumer Affairs); not on the State debarment list and/or have had issues with a respective

County, City and County of Honolulu, in this case; and continue to remain an entity registered to do business in Hawai'i (Alaska and/or on the Continental U.S.);

16) Ensuring that the organizations for funding meet the appropriate zoning and permitting requirements (fire and building code);

17) Examining whether or not applicants have the management team and staff to complete a project or service in an expedited and timely fashion;

18) Implementing a review process that ensures the participating jurisdiction that the agency's organizational objectives do not conflict with HUD's mandates for services, and housing for low- and moderate-income persons;

19) Mandating that prospective and granted non-profits complete training and seminars on proper reporting, use, financial disclosure of federal funds (these seminars should be completed on a quarterly and/or semiannual basis to

ensure that agencies understand their reporting requirements, federal audit requirements, necessity of preparing clear and concise financial reports, file documentation, schedule for monitoring, et. al.;

20) Notifying not-for-profits in advance that the procurement process is set to begin and then mandating that they meet with the participating jurisdiction to ensure that they understand their rights, responsibilities and legal obligations to HUD;

21) Establishing a process for suspending contracts for projects (service or contractual) and/or agencies that are unable to complete their contractual, procurement, permitting, environmental and labor requirements in a timely fashion, have misrepresented their project or otherwise;

22) Increasing the monitoring conducted for not-for-profits to occur on a quarterly basis in order to ensure that agencies are meeting their contractual requirements, including

reporting and documentation, compliance with federal law, etc.;

23) Final payment closeout shall be changed from a process that incorporates only a cursory review of invoices at or near the end of the contract closeout process to one that has quarterly invoice and deliverable reviews, in order to identify problems with the contract prior to its overall completion when the window to address complicated issues has passed and avoid the current procedure and response, which only withholds final payment (that typically represents only 10 to 20% of the overall contract) and provides very little incentive for the recipient to modify their procedures or change their conduct; and

24) Payments shall clearly spell out the services that are being rendered, the salaries, fringe benefits and indirect costs that employees are receiving and any equipment or supplies that organizations are acquiring. A description of what the jurisdiction is purchasing shall be clearly spelled out in the corresponding written section of the invoice. Each

accounting line item shall be accompanied by a substantial written description detailing the exact services provided and/or what the employees assigned to those FTEs accomplished during the invoicing period.

The guidelines above can be utilized for new affordable house construction and existing structures compliance. How can these twenty-four guidelines be implemented and executed from a business perspective more effectively?

The answer is simple. It requires an independent third-party audit on a quarterly basis (i.e. one of large big-four auditors or a smaller firm with no-conflicts of interest) and again on an annual basis. It also requires a building inspector and social services review on a similar timeline. Findings must be remediated with service providers including loan documents, receipts and building permits to demonstrate that the structure's plumbing and electrical work has been repaired and any propane and gas lines have been tested for leaks.

Included are some photos of a project that remediates some of the issues with deferred maintenance, providing a model for property oversight.

Proper property repairs being executed by the author to a windowsill with significant dry rot from insect damage.

The author is wearing proper safety equipment, including a respirator designed to offset exposure to lead dust and VOCs, gloves and long-sleeve clothing. In major siding repairs I recommend wearing a DuPont® Tyvek® suit, and full respirator mask with a face shield or goggles. This work demonstrates good execution of a problematic housing issue that should not be transferred to tenants under any circumstances, due to safety risks and health compliance. This is the responsibility of the property manager. A periodic and comprehensive audit can uncover these types of issues and is worth the expense and time involved.

Why? Good property managers proactively address jobsite problems and tackle the problems head-on. Incompetent property managers take a defensive approach, deferring maintenance and repair, until there are dangerous health and safety issues involved.

The final result is both rewarding and profitable for an ethical property manager. It delivers an excellent product resulting in housing at full capacity, maintaining a healthy bottom-line and resulting a positive net-income, particularly if the housing units are owned by large scale Wall Street conglomerates or hedge funds.

Finished on-site product.

Actuary risk formulas that utilize cost-benefit formulas that only factor potential payouts from hospital visits and repairs due to deferring property maintenance and restorations as long as possible are unnecessary. They are the result of grossly incompetent property managers that have no real-world construction experience. They have failed to account for how a simple, small experienced maintenance team can complete the majority of repairs in a cost-effective, efficient and timely manner, far below what the actuary tables actually suggest (i.e. cost of payouts from a class-action lawsuit suit versus regular maintenance). Investors should steer clear from these myopic investment teams employed by Wall-street firms or hedge funds that own large tracts of affordable housing. They have failed to understand how simple and effective maintenance can result in a thriving property, creating a positive multiplier effect throughout the community. A well-maintained property results in new businesses in the surrounding neighborhood. This is based on basic supply and demand. I highly recommend a consulting team (for any corporate conglomerate) conduct a new property review to re-evaluate a property's profitability and revenue streams.

2nd series of finished on-site product.

Selection Process

Federal programs to stimulate low- and moderate-income housing rely on some the most burdensome and complex regulations around. The formulas outlined in this chapter provide guidance on why more developers avoid building more affordable housing.

They build apartment complexes with one goal in mind: maximizing profits. They have no other goals. They are not concerned about a development's impact on the surrounding community (traffic, infrastructure, public works) or any other aspect of the development.

Initiatives nominated as a part of industry and private sector procurement processes (that integrate public funding) need to engage in stringent due diligence in order to be selected and complete their projects successfully:

Understanding that the procurement, contracting, billing, financial underwriting, permitting and other deadlines integral to utilizing federal, state or county funds is essential (i.e. that the timelines for finalizing these processes may be delayed by utilizing government funding).

If U.S. Department of Housing and Urban Development (HUD) funds are used then there may be certain restrictions regarding the use of those funds that limit the types of activities that can occur in those housing developments, community centers or building renovation projects (as they are targeted for low- and moderate income persons, areas, et. al.).

Limiting factors may include, but are not confined to, the requirement that a certain percentage of a housing project's residents be low- and moderate-income persons (or that a certain percentage of community center users within a specified Census Tract be low- and moderate-income persons). Private developers that are working with government agencies should be aware of these restrictions when they partner with government agencies in order to complete a project in a timely and cost-effective manner.

Government purchasing processes do not necessarily provide a guaranteed source of financing for housing construction projects developed in partnership with government and private industry. The procurement process may not result in the direct awarding of funds to a developer.

U.S. Department of Housing and Urban Development, under its HOME program, requires that housing projects (small-, mid- and large-scale construction ventures) adhere to specific cost allocation principles. The guidelines outlined below work well for new construction, but are much more challenging for retrofitting existing high-rise structures or complexes.

a.	For example a private developer or not-for-profit must take into consideration that if they have applied for government HOME funds that represent thirty (30%) percent of the total eligible project costs, they must ensure that thirty (30%) of units in that structure are HOME assisted.

b.	Additionally, a private developer must also determine the minimum home units and the maximum home investment that government funds will allow. It is important to note that these examples are based in part on Hawai'i numbers.

  i.	A **Cost Test** is compared to a **Subsidy Limit Test** to determine the maximum government (HUD - HOME) investment in a specific project.

  ii.	**Cost Test ("Fair-Share") – Maximum HOME Investment** is derived as follows:

   Step 1: Example:

The total eligible costs are $4,000,000, Total units include 40 comparable units, HOME units include 16 units and the 221(d)(3) limit is $157,446 (one-bedroom subsidy limit for 2015).

Step 1: HOME units = HOME unit %

Total Units

Step 2: HOME Unit % x Total Eligible Costs =
**"Fair Share" HOME Maximum Dollar ($)
Investment**

Fair Share Test	
Total eligible costs	$4,000,000
HOME Units	16
Comparable Units	40
Maximum Investment	0.4
221(d)(3) - 2011	$157,446
	$1,600,000

iii. A **Subsidy Limit Test – Maximum Dollar ($)
Investment** is derived as follows:

Step 1: Example:

The total eligible costs are $4,000,000, Total units include 40 comparable units, HOME units include 16 units and the 221(d)(3) limit is $157,466 (one-bedroom subsidy limit for 2015).

Step 2:   Number (#) of HOME Units x HOME Subsidy Limit = Total HOME Subsidy Limit

Comparable Unit -	
Subsidy Limit Test	
HOME Units	16
221(d)(3) - 2011	$157,466
	$2,519,456

iv. Conclusion – The maximum government investment under HUD's HOME program (or "Fair-Share" investment) equals the lesser financial amount derived by calculating and comparing the cost test to the subsidy limit test. In this example, the maximum investment would be $1,600,000, the lesser of $2,519,456 and $1,600,000. This formula is executed in the most efficient manner when applied to new housing construction. It is less efficient and harder to apply to an existing residential property.

v. The formula is as follows: The minimum number (#) of HOME units is determined by comparing a cost test to a subsidy test and taking the greater number (#) of the two calculations.

vi. **Cost Test ("Fair-Share") – Minimum Number (#) of Units** - is derived as follows:

Step 1:   Example:

The total project cost is $10,000,000, HOME Investment is $4,000,000, 40 comparable units, # HOME units required to be calculated, the 221(d)(3) limit is $157,466 (one-bedroom subsidy limit for 2015).

Step 2:   HOME Investment

Total Eligible Costs = HOME Investment %

Step 3:   HOME Investment % x Total Units =

"Fair Share" HOME Units

Fair Share Test	
Total project cost	$10,000,000
HOME Investment	$4,000,000
	0.4
Comparable Units	40
221(d)(3) - 2011	$157,446
Minimum Units	16

vii. A **Subsidy Limit Test – Minimum Number (#) of Units** is derived as follows:

Step 1:   Example:

The total project cost is $10,000,000, HOME Investment is $4,000,000, 40 comparable units, therefore the number of HOME units required to be calculated under the 221(d)(3) limit is $157,456 (one-bedroom subsidy limit for 2015).

Step 2:   HOME Investment

Maximum Subsidy Limit = **221(d)(3) Units**

Comparable Unit -	
Subsidy Limit Test	
HOME Investment	$4,000,000
221(d)(3) - 2011	$157,456
Minimum Units	25

viii. Conclusion – The minimum HOME Units under HUD's HOME program (or "Fair-Share" investment) equals the greater number of units derived by calculating and comparing the cost test to the subsidy limit test. In this example, the minimum number of HOME units would be 25, or the larger number of 16 and 25.

ix. The conclusion is different when calculating non-comparable units (the above calculation) is utilized by government agencies and private entities when conducting a comparable unit analysis.

c. Additionally, a private developer must also determine the minimum home units and the maximum home investment that government funds will allow (from a non-comparable unit standpoint).

i. **Cost Test ("Fair-Share") –Maximum Investment – Non-Comparable Units** - is derived as follows:

Step 1: Example:

The total project eligible cost is $10,000,000, Cost for HOME units is $4,000,000, Common costs are $400,000, 40 non-comparable units, HOME units is 25, Total unit square footage is 12,000, and the HOME square footage is 6,000; therefore the 221(d)(3) limit is $157,446 (one-bedroom subsidy limit for 2015).

How to determine the maximum HOME investment?

Step 2:   HOME Square Ft

Total square feet of all units = HOME Square Feet %

Step 3:   HOME Square Feet % x Total Eligible Common Costs = HOME Share of Common Costs.

Maximum HOME Investment	
Fair Share Test	
Non-Comparable Units	
HOME Square Feet	6,000
Total Square Feet - All Units	12,000
HOME Square Feet %	0.5
HOME Square Feet %	0.5
Total Eligible Common Costs	$400,000
HOME Share of Common Costs	$200,000
HOME Share of Common Costs	$4,000,000
HOME Unit Eligible Costs	$400,000
"Fair Share" of Total	$4,400,000
221(d)(3) - 2011	$157,446
Maximum Investment	$4,400,000

ii. A **Subsidy Limit Test – Maximum HOME Investment** is derived as follows:

Step 1: Example:

The total project eligible cost is $10,000,000, Cost for HOME units is $4,000,000, the common costs are $400,000, with 40 non-comparable units, the number of HOME units is 25, Total unit square footage is 12,000, and HOME square footage is 6,000; therefore the 221(d)(3) limit is $157,446 (one-bedroom subsidy limit for 2015).

How to determine the maximum HOME investment?

Step 2: HOME Share of Common Costs + HOME Unit Eligible Costs = **"Fair share" of total**

Subsidy Limit Test	
Non-Comparable Units	
HOME Units	25
221(d)(3) - 2011	$157,466
Maximum Investment	$3,936,150

iii. Conclusion – The maximum government investment under HUD's HOME program (or "Fair-Share" investment, non-comparable units) equals the lesser financial amount derived by calculating and comparing the cost test to the subsidy limit test. In this example, the maximum investment would be $3,936,150, the lesser of $3,936,150 and $4,400,000.

This subset of the operations of one of HUD's programs (the HOME program) demonstrates the complexity of this particular program and illustrates the difficulty that developers face when utilizing federal funds for a housing development project, particularly one that impacts low- and moderate-income persons. The dynamics of financing a housing project change significantly when it is a private development financed by banks and private equity and insured by for-profit insurance agencies. *However*, developing a project that can be designed, procured, financed, built and operative doesn't change regardless of whether government funding is or is not included.

iv. Developers are also challenged by income limit restrictions with respect to the development of low- and moderate-income housing. For example, the HUD HOME program defines two specific categories of income for tenants:

a. Very Low Income (VLI) is typically set at 50% of median (set at different thresholds for 1, 2, 3 - 8 person households – i.e. a staggered scale, $21K, $24K, et. al.); and

b. Low Income (LI) is defined as 80% (tiered scale) of median.

c. Note: For initial occupancy, 60% of median (again set as a staggered range) is an acceptable standard for HOME rental properties.

d. Developers must include the appropriate mix of low and high HOME, fair market rent and other rent limits depending on the size and funding scope of their projects.

e. Private developers face issues with planning and permitting, zoning, utility easements, parking, roadway access issues, bonding, insurance, demolition (if applicable), construction, renovating and/or retrofitting a facility, landscaping, street construction, signage installation, inspections and certificates of occupancy.

f. Private developers typically must work with private lenders and other equity financers to underwrite their projects.

g. Insurance companies provide various forms of bonds for construction projects. For example with performance bonds the parties involved will perform and complete the construction work.

Conclusion

This extensive example of how affordable housing funding can work illustrates the complexity that developers face when they attempt to integrate affordable housing measures into their projects, particularly multi-story high rises. The mechanics of how federal guidelines work is exceedingly cumbersome. Developers also have very little incentive to build anything other than luxury housing, which maximizes their profits.

As many multi-unit structures are bundled into conglomerates and owned by hedge funds and money managers, they also are only interested in profits (nothing else). When fund managers do own affordable federal housing projects they are riddled with neglect and problems.

Hawai'i's public housing projects for many years had no hot water.[51] Unfortunately this type of neglect is the norm, not the exception. It is true regardless of whether the housing is managed by public or private institutions.

---

[51] *Deplorable living conditions at Mayor Wright Housing result in settlement for tenants.* Hawaii News Now. March 11, 2015. http://www.hawaiinewsnow.com/story/28363868/deplorable-living-conditions-at-mayor-wright-housing-result-in-settlement-for-tenants.

With private institutions (as the lead owners) the situation can be even worse, due to limited government oversight. The solution lies in increasing the housing supply beyond demand.

The challenge is overcoming the regulatory hurdles to developing new high rises; and building high-rise structures that create a diverse mix of affordability not isolated islands of low- and moderate-income communities that are segregated from group at large.

Mixed use housing that combines commercial and industrial spaces, along with parks and open spaces and a range of income levels actually strengthens a community. It does so by creating healthier urban populations that are not forced to commute as far to their workplaces. The residents and employers are able to walk or cycle to work and are more physically fit, reducing their health costs and general sick days. This is a direct and tangible benefit to employers, large and small because health insurance premiums fall, as fewer people need medical services and hospital visits. For those employers that pay a portion of their employees' health plans, this cost savings is significant. It translates into direct bottom-line savings and profitability. For publicly traded companies this can translate into greater shareholder returns.

For private equity companies, a focus on underwriting and investing in technologies that can innovate the energy and water use of these highly dense urban hubs is more than critical. It is essential. Property managers and residents save money and time from innovations that reduce the electricity and water usage, while creating more productive environments. Investors receive a direct return, maximizing their profits.

The Modernization of the World's Infrastructure

Airports

For a comprehensive analysis it is critical to utilize parcel data, Tax Map Keys or a World Airport Code when identifying a specific airport, runway, maintenance and fuel stations, hangers or other facilities that require extensive upgrades. An examination of the existing infrastructure and zoning is essential to the modernization of these systems.

Why is this the case?

Each municipality is unique. Every country has its own rules and regulations. All airports were built with different space allotments, ability to expand their operations, modernize their runways and a multitude of other factors. Airports that have added monorails, subway extensions to provide service to their existing mass transit programs are in-line to innovate.

San Francisco International Airport (SFO) and Oakland International Airport (OAK) have BART extensions, with OAK adding this feature more recently.

Included below is an image of the process of traveling from SFO to Richmond (or one of the neighboring BART locations). Upon arrival at SFO one exits the airport through a tram/monorail. Then at a connecting part station (Civic Center, Market, et. al.) passengers are able to connect to one of the outlying suburbs, like Richmond.

Transit from SFO to tram to BART to Richmond.

Why is this important?

Regional transit systems need to be expanded further into the suburban areas, adding additional lines and providing a full schedule of maintenance and period replacement of cars, station improvements and even adding additional lines that run perpendicular to existing track. Municipal bond offerings are still a traditional method of financing these upgrades and repairs.

Funding Mechanisms and Regulatory Oversight of Airports

Airports in the United States are need of serious repairs and upgrades. An examination of airports in China and other parts of the world reveal infrastructure with long runways, modernized terminals and innovative building design.

Airports in the United States are funded (in part) through the following:

(1) "The Airport Improvement Program (AIP) provides grants to public agencies — and, in some cases, to private owners and entities -- for the planning and development of public-use airports that are included in the National Plan of Integrated Airport Systems (NPIAS)."[52]

---

[52]What is AIP? Federal Aviation Administration. 2017.

(2) "The Airport and Airway Trust Fund (AATF) was created by the Airport and Airway Revenue Act of 1970, and provides funding for the federal commitment to the nation's aviation system through several aviation-related excise taxes."[53]

Government funding is not enough. It requires private industry to step forward and partner with the aviation industry to build airline hubs that met the demands of larger planes and other aviation innovations.

The U.S. aviation industry is facing essential macro-level issues with modernization (aging facilities, lack of integrated hubs). How these issues are defined, funded and executed will define the competitiveness of the United States for generations to come.

---

https://www.faa.gov/airports/aip/overview/.
[53] Airport & Airway Trust Fund (AATF). 2017. https://www.faa.gov/about/budget/aatf/.

Infrastructure Upgrade, Inc.® supports the modernization of infrastructure through the promotion of innovative design in architecture, engineering and planning and partnerships with private industry to build state of the art facilities that integrate high-speed rail facilities, subways, trams, highways and housing.

Railroads

Railroads in the United States are in serious need of expansion. CSX Transportation, Union Pacific Railroad, Norfolk Southern Railway all rely on track that requires maintenance, upgrades and even replacement. The longer these major providers wait to invest in track and new cars the more expensive they become in the future.

When I have walked down in close proximity to industrial and commuter railroad tracks in California, New York and other parts of the country, the infrastructure is worn, the cars clearly show their age and use. It is an industry that is one of the backbones of the U.S. economy. New cars, tracks, rail crossings and computer technology systems are needed for the transit sector as a whole. Years of infrastructure backlogs have impacted the quality of these operations; creating significant risks to both the workers and the communities that rail runs through.

Government Regulatory Bodies and Funding

Railroad development in the United State is funded (in part) through the United States Department of Transportation, Federal Railroad Administration's programs, including, but not limited to, the Passenger Rail Investment and Improvement Act of 2008 (PRIIA) and more recently the American Recovery and Reinvestment Act of 2009 (Recovery Act or ARRA).

Railroad highway crossing improvements in the United States are funded under Title 23--Highways Chapter I--Federal Highway Administration, Department of Transportation Part 646--Railroads--Table of Contents Subpart B--Railroad-Highway Projects Sec. 646.208 Funding: "(a) Railroad/highway crossing projects may be funded through the Federal-aid funding source appropriate for the involved project."

An example of commuter rail transit is shown in Antioch, California.

Transit improvements must come from a combination of Federal, state and local regulatory authorities, funding in tandem with private enterprise.

Most importantly the private sector must step forward to try and develop transit solutions in tandem with government. This is what the Hyperloop One® is doing with its ultra fast rail technologies.

Maintaining a Competitive Edge in a Global Economy

Railroad upgrades and new rail line installations are critical for connecting people and commerce. Railroad improvements need to be completed in an economical fashion, designed to integrate a community, not circumvent it. To be viable railroads need to connect all population centers, not begin or end as isolated hubs (particularly if they are financed through bonds that a state or municipal government issues in partnership with an accredited underwriter) and only a portion of the State or municipality's population benefits from their development because they would have to drive or be transported to the rail hubs to utilize them.

According to the Economist Magazine's September 24, 2011 Special Report article *Commodities: Crowded Out* "It takes years to find and develop new mines and oil reservoirs and to build the infrastructure (rigs, pipelines, railways, ports) to bring the commodities to market. Supply responds slowly to price increases and delay often leads to excessive investment which then depresses prices."[54] This capacity expansion continues to lag in the U.S.

This article highlights the need to maintain and improve functioning rail systems that can support industries that are critical to maintaining a competitive edge, particularly for the United States, as emerging markets like China and India become more and more dominant globally.[55]

---

[54]Commodities. Crowded out. Sep 24th 2011.
http://www.economist.com/node/21528986.
[55]Harlem Subway Derailment Snarls Commute. WSJ. August 27, 2017. https://www.wsj.com/articles/harlem-subway-derailment-snarls-commute-1498577676.

Nearly seven (7) years later very little has changed. The United States is still not competitive in the global marketplace. It still doesn't have a coast-to-coast rail system. Almost every other industrialized nation has high-speed rail, including China, which like the United States has a large landmass to provide service for rail hubs and transit centers spur developments, housing and new job growth. New technologies exist that have made high-speed rail more competitive, driving the costs and installation down.

Steel on steel rail is fine for industrial transport of timber, coal, iron-ore, minerals, cattle and other large weight commodities.

These systems can be modernized to make rail in the United States more viable with the rest of the world, providing a great economic expansion strategy.

NYC's recent rail problems, which necessitated that the governor of New York declare a state of emergency, directly highlight how disruptive mass-transit has become to one of the world's largest hubs of economic activity.[56] The New York City system is nearly one hundred years old and necessitated a $1 billion influx of capital to resolve its disruption of service and recent accident in June of 2017, which injured nearly forty people.[57]

A recent trip on the GG train line from Brooklyn to Grand Central highlights how crowded the transit system has become. As I boarded the train, people were hitting the side of the subway car in frustration. After the train departed from the station, we waited for twenty-five (25) minutes in the sweltering heat underground. By the time the train started to move again tensions in the car were palpable with riders beginning to joke nervously and then complain.

---

[56]Emma G. Fitzsimmons. Cuomo Declares a State of Emergency for New York City Subways. June 29, 2017.
https://www.nytimes.com/2017/06/29/nyregion/cuomo-declares-a-state-of-emergency-for-the-subway.html?rref=collection%2Fsectioncollection%2Fnyregion&action=click&contentCollection=nyregion&region=rank&module=package&version=highlights&contentPlacement=7&pgtype=sectionfront.
[57]*Id.*

GG Train from Brooklyn to New York, New York.

Why is having safe, secure and *on time* transit systems and infrastructure so important? The operations of industry are disrupted when employees are unable to get to work punctually. Industries are unable to expand their businesses easily when commuters can't access their offices. It makes it difficult for companies to expand their operations, making them less competitive in the global marketplace.

Infrastructure Improvements; and Economic and Gross Domestic Product (GDP) Improvements

The November 21, 2011 issue of Fortune Magazine's article *Rebuilding Roads and Rails* which includes an interview with Matt Rose, CEO of Burlington Northern Railroad notes that "The U.S. has fallen from 8 to 16 on the World Economic Forum's infrastructure rating; one bipartisan report cites a $200 billion annual shortfall just to maintain our current transportation network. But in these tight economic times, who's going to pay?"[58] The debate over who is going to pay for infrastructure improvements continues in 2017. It hasn't been solved by cooperative policymaking, which is one of the hallmarks of democracy, not a secondary after-thought. True policy making should focus on infrastructure and building cost effective and efficient communities and great businesses.

---

[58]Nina Easton. America's infrastructure is sorely lacking. Matt Rose, CEO of Burlington Northern Railroad, offers solutions. Fortune. November 11, 2011. http://fortune.com/2011/11/11/how-to-rebuild-our-nations-roads-and-rails/.

The current leadership of the United States is extraordinarily myopic. Their claim to be sound financial policy makers has no basis in fact. The longer it takes to resolve infrastructure funding, the higher the cost of materials and labor (inflation directly impacts these items) and cost of borrowing money increases (interest rates rise).

In 2017 there have been no visionary or infrastructure projects of any note in the United States, with the exception of Elon Musk's Hyperloop One (that is still in the development phase) and the attempts to finalize California's high speed rail from Los Angeles to San Francisco.

Other municipalities that have embarked on expensive projects are using antiquated technologies, like steel-on-steel rail. For example, the Honolulu rail is facing an up to a three (3) billion dollar shortfall, despite local, state and federal financing because it is using elevated stations and antiquated rail technologies instead of new lightweight systems.[59]

---

[59]Cathy Bussewitz. *Honolulu Tests Rail Car on Track for First Time.* The Associated Press. May 30, 2017.
https://www.usnews.com/news/best-states/hawaii/articles/2017-05-30/honolulu-tests-rail-car-on-track-for-first-time.

Infrastructure investment is an economic multiplier creating jobs and directly providing stimulus to the economy. However, a greater level of accountability for civil works projects is required. The permitting and environmental process needs to be streamlined. Federal agencies providing oversight over public works must be simplified.

Increasing tolls on U.S. roads and bridges, along with a gas tax increase, would create a revenue stream for government in direct partnership with private industry. Money can also be added from private hedge funds and additional government bonds. Government bonds provide low-cost solutions to financing infrastructure improvements, but infrastructure banks, including those that China has developed, are executing projects in places as diverse as Africa (within countries like Nigeria). This model of an infrastructure bank can and should be implemented in the United States. It shouldn't replace municipal bonds (or bonds in general). Instead they will act as a supplementary mechanism.

The Lake Merritt project (that I documented below extensively) is an example of a bond measure that was used (in part) to finance the construction of construction and estuary restoration.

This project was voted upon and passed as Measure DD by Oakland voters, which includes $198.25 million in financing for roads, bridges, estuary restoration and other improvements.[60]

An infrastructure bank, similar to the Federal Reserve System, with a head institution and regional banks can be used to set and implement infrastructure policy and financing. Monetary policy will still come from the Federal Reserve, adjusting interest rates to address natural inflation rates of goods and services. An Infrastructure Bank will work in partnership with the Federal Reserve, setting infrastructure policy based in part on monetary rates, providing streamlined and efficient programs to stimulate the economy through underwriters (banks) and government working in partnership local communities.

---

[60]*Oakland's Measure DD*. WaterFront Action. 2017. http://www.waterfrontaction.org/dd/index.htm.

Lake Merritt, California road, park and waterway improvements in progress.

I spent an extensive amount of time tracking and documenting this venture. It was easy to record because I would run loops around the perimeter of Lake Merritt, often running into the team at Pandora®. The more comprehensive the street improvements became, the more visitors the region attracted. This was one of the most striking aspects of this project.

In 2017 the operations of the U.S government have not been streamlined in a significant fashion despite the current administration's efforts.

At Infrastructure Upgrade, Inc.® we encourage streamlining the federal agencies with oversight over infrastructure, simplify the permitting and environmental process for large scale construction projects, placing additional tolls on roads and bridges to increase revenue to fund these initiatives and issuing strategic bonds to provide further financing.

Bridges as a Physical and Conceptual Connector

The flying buttress was created in the age of enlightenment and was designed to support the outside of buildings. The visual shape of the buttress has been reinterpreted and incorporated as the underlying support of a bridge.

Conceptually the wooden slats of a bridge are the connector of communities, linking them physically and mentally. Bridge building teaches groups the power of teamwork. From a psychological perspective a bridge that has been built represents a passage to another country or community, creating an opportunity for the exchange of ideas, commerce and people. The rope handrails on a primitive bridge represent the safety net that keeps the population in this focal point of exchange on track. Bridge building is more than a metaphor. The flying buttress and other later technological engineering developments are the stimulus that has shaped the very fabric of society, while creating the bridge to the future.

Government Deregulation and Creating Economies of Scale and Efficiencies in Maintaining and Upgrading Infrastructure

The future of energy production lies in the deregulation of government regulated industries. Roadways, utilities and other industries can operate in an efficient and cost effective manner while continuing to provide the regulated services that are necessary to operate.

Are government subsidies the exclusive answer to promoting renewable energy growth? Manufacturing capacity must be expanded to reduce the cost of producing these technologies.

How should these initiatives be paid for? Increasing the fuel tax, adding a small development fee percentage to the sales tax in multiple states or through a combination of venture capital, private equity and debt?

How do we create a business model that develops transmission infrastructure (that allows more users onto the grid) to be financed and built?

Distributed energy that supplements power and utility distribution requirements at a more localized level can begin to address the cost and safety issues associated with aging transmission infrastructure.

This type of energy allocation can be a viable solution for small to mid-sized communities.

Independent 3rd Party Power Production

An example of distributed energy projects is a six and half (6½) megawatt project that is going to generate electricity from wood recovered from waste material. In municipalities around the United States (and the world) there are thousands of tons of waste material that are sent to landfills. There are landfills that accept trash and those that take construction and demolition (C&D) debris. When a building is demolished (or a store is redesigned) this construction and demolition material goes to the C&D landfill. A large percentage of C&D material is wood (up to 50%) Pyrolysis involves taking C&D wood and removing the metal and non-wood materials, shredding and then heating the scraps in the absence of oxygen to create a synthetic natural gas from the wood's hydrocarbons. The gas that is generated from this process is then burned in a boiler producing stream, which rotates a turbine to generate electricity. The electricity that is generated through this process must be connected to the grid by the local utility and distributed to businesses and consumers for power. This process is classified as renewable energy because it is non-fossil fuel based.

Treating Medical Waste with Pyrolysis

This process is also used for treating medical and low-level radioactive waste. For example, as a part of day-to-day operations at a nuclear facility: every day the workers at the plant wear protective clothing and these materials need to be disposed of properly. (This same scenario occurs if there is a nuclear accident.) If you consider overalls and other clothing that are partially radioactive these materials can't just be taken to a landfill.

This hazardous material is placed in the pyrolysis system and it removes all the moisture and all the hydrocarbons. This leaves up to 10% of the original volume. Medical providers use this type of system because of the high disposal costs of low-level radioactive waste.

The technology in this specific process uses the heat from a recovery boiler to make steam. The stream is used to operate a sterilizer (an autoclave) to purify a portion of the waste material. A segment of the waste requires high thermal destruction and a portion of it requires heating from steam. It is energy efficient because we take the excess heat to make the steam.

It is important to note the 10% of concentrated waste that is generated, as a part of this process is still highly toxic. It must be disposed of properly, as it can leach into water systems and impact human health. It requires at a minimum a specially lined landfill.

It is also important to emphasis that under no circumstances can this process be used to treat high-level radioactive spent reactor fuel, which is highly unstable and very toxic.

This process typically requires using thermal batteries (with salt), to store electricity. This is a challenge for pyrolysis, distributed energy or solar panels. If a business seeks to be off the grid, batteries provide a reliable source of power particularly when it is raining or there is no wind.

Fiber Optic Capacity & Telecommunications

An area of concern that warrants improvement is the need for fiber optic infrastructure upgrades. New fiber optic cable installations can reduce the need for vehicle and air traffic for work, allowing in some instances a cost effective mechanism for businesses to communicate with one another.

Infrastructure Upgrade® recommends that these fiber optic installations be tied into other utility work (including water, wastewater and electric improvements) in order to complete the process in a cost effective and efficient manner.

Solar Power Subsidies and Equitable Power Distribution

As more customers install photovoltaic panels on their homes and businesses (with associated net metering agreements with utilities) those customers that are left on the grid assume higher costs that the utility passes on to them. This issue has led to the dissolution of regulatory frameworks.

Infrastructure Upgrade® supports more localized distributed energy solutions that require lower capitalization and can reduce distribution and transmission costs by providing electricity closer to the source of use.

PG&E current power content distribution (2011 to 2016 comparison) is as follows:

Energy Resources	PG&E 2011 Power Mix	PG&E 2016 Power Mix[61]
Eligible Renewable:	19%	33%
Biomass and waste	4%	
Geothermal	5%	
Small hydroelectric	4%	
Solar	0%	
Wind	6%	
Coal	0%	
Large Hydroelectric	18%	12%
Natural Gas	25%	17%
Nuclear	22%	24%
Other	1%	
Unspecified	15%	13%
Total	100%	100%

---

[61]Exploring Clean Energy Solutions. PG&E. 2017.
https://www.pge.com/en_US/about-pge/environment/what-we-are-doing/clean-energy-solutions/clean-energy-solutions.page.

One of the critical questions of the future: is it economically feasible for a power utility to shift its power mix over time while maintaining its competitive edge? The corporations and governments that solve this question in an efficient and cost effective manner will emerge as the business leaders of the next generation.

Data Barns and Their Impact on Regional & Global Power Demand

There is a myth of data centers reducing the country's footprint on energy usage and the environment. Nothing could be further from the truth.

The New York Times® in James Glanz's article *Power, Pollution and the Internet* outlines the impact that data centers that Facebook®, Yahoo!®, Google®, Microsoft®, Apple®, Amazon®, Salesforce® and other global industry leaders utilize "use about 30 billion watts of electricity, roughly equivalent to the output of 30 nuclear power plants, according to estimates industry analysts compiled for The Times."[62]

---

[62]James Glanz. *Power, Pollution and the Internet*. The New York Times. September 22, 2012.

This has increased to "about 70 billion kilowatt-hours of electricity in 2014 (the most recent year examined) representing 2 percent of the country's total energy consumption."[63]

Data centers have appeared on California's Toxic Air Contaminant Inventory due to their use of diesel generators to provide backup power to their systems.

Additionally, "Nationwide, data centers used about 76 billion kilowatt-hours in 2010, or roughly 2 percent of all electricity used in the country that year" contrasted with the paper industry that uses "67 billion kilowatt-hours from the grid in 2010."[64]

This issue conflicts with the myth that the computer industry is less resource intensive because it has reduced the volume of paper being used. Instead the industry's impact is more resource intensive than ever imagined.

---

http://www.nytimes.com/2012/09/23/technology/data-centers-waste-vast-amounts-of-energy-belying-industry-image.html.
[63]*Id.*
[64]*Id.*

A balance needs to be achieved. Data centers are unlikely to go away in the future. Instead they will become more prevalent as companies like Amazon®, Apple® and Microsoft® expand their product and service offerings.

Infrastructure Upgrade, Inc.® uses a combination of metal and cloud based servers all of which use electricity to power its mobile solutions.

I strongly recommend that this industry take steps to improve the energy efficiency of their industry, supplementing their diesel power generator use with photovoltaic, wind and other power sources.

If this industry is only using 6 to 12 percent of the energy that they draw from, then there is certainly room for them to improve the efficiency of their services and save money over the long-term. Additionally, the payback period for installing a large-scale photovoltaic system (via an amortization schedule) creates a very advantageous investment for corporations that are seeking to reduce their power consumption. Infrastructure Upgrade, Inc.® recommends that this industry take two steps: (1) Improve the efficiency of their operations; and (2) Install supplemental power generation sources and negotiate power purchase agreements with the regional utility (PG&E®, for example) to reduce their impact on the grid nationwide.

The cloud will be the future but it can and should be a system that is powered in a more sophisticated fashion.

Having worked on moving a major data center operation from Monterrey Park, California to Omaha, Nebraska and Denver, Colorado (disaster recovery) for a major bank, I can attest that the operations can be consolidated and made more energy efficient.

Data Farms and Their Impact on Surrounding Communities

Many data centers during their inception relied on diesel generators to keep their operations continuously operating, with harmful impacts on the surrounding communities that house them. Under pressure from activist groups companies have shifted their power matrix to renewables.

For example, both Apple® and Google® have shifted their data center operations energy requirements to ensure that they have the right to purchase electricity from renewable energy sources for their operations throughout the world.

It is unlikely that cloud services will disappear in the near future. However, data farms that power cloud web services can be designed in a more sustainable fashion, that allow the companies to improve energy efficiency, backup their systems and reduce their impact on the surrounding community both in terms of emissions and competing power use.

At Infrastructure Upgrade, Inc.® we use both Apple® and Google® products, both designing applications to work on their platforms and app stores.

Bio-Fuel Plants and Their Impact on the Environment and Surrounding Communities

The rise in U.S. government subsidies for bio-fuel plants has had a direct impact on the environment and communities in the surrounding vicinity. Bio-fuel plants are categorized in many cases as a source of power that is environmentally progressive because they do not rely on extractive fossil fuels to provide power (coal, oil, et. al.). Wood-fired plants are not a panacea in terms of their impact within the communities that surround them. Carbon-based emissions are one of the direct impacts. There is always a cost and a benefit to using a particular technology to generate power.

The power sources of the future should strive to be more innovative, localized and utilize technologies that reduce their environmental footprint, save money, increase efficiency and serve their customers. The utilities of the future will be smaller, nimble, flexible and transferable across multiple communities. Utilities should develop research and development units to promote the future of energy generation, much in the way Bell Labs® served as a critical source of new innovations in technology. There is always a cost and a benefit of generating power, but this cost can be minimized by constantly striving to be innovative.

Government Subsidies and Their Impact on Market Distortion

Government subsidies do distort the adoption of technologies that would otherwise not be cost-effective or even be brought to market. Subsidizing wind and solar power do not change the underlying unaffordable nature of the technologies. Taxpayers continue to underwrite them through government programs, instead of the manufacturers of renewables.

The market needs to develop technologies as a by-product of corporate research rather than super-imposing subsidies to the extent that they allow technologies that aren't the most cost effective to enter the marketplace. Bell Labs® is the classic example of a corporate research and development facility that spawned multiple innovations. The large utilities need to develop research and development arms to promote this type of innovation in the marketplace, rather than having government attempt to introduce the innovation through financing. The net result is technologies that are more cost effective and efficient when they are developed by corporate research and development rather than government programs and policies.

Flooding and its Potential to Impact the Pipelines of Utilities

Flooding has always been an issue for communities because of its potential to damage infrastructure and disrupt local and regional markets. As the infrastructure in communities ages floods have the potential to damage or break gas, oil, electric, water and wastewater pipelines causing costly maintenance and repair issues.

After Hurricane Sandy flooded New York City companies of all sizes moved their electrical systems from the basements to a higher level. This approach should be used as the model for future proactivity.

The records highlight a gap in regulations that could negatively impact pipelines buried beneath rivers nationwide.

Governments and utilities should take an active approach and begin the process of upgrading water and wastewater pipelines and other utility infrastructure now. The cost of investing now is less (in real dollars) when factoring in inflation and the future cost of underwriting these projects.

Investing in New Energy Infrastructure

New energy infrastructure investments are needed, particularly in the area of natural gas and other traditional energy infrastructure. Natural gas as a significant source of energy has increased in the United States.

It is a cleaner technology and can be developed within the United States, reducing our reliance on imported petroleum and spawning new jobs and economic growth.

Energy buying cooperatives and aggregation are a strategy that can be utilized by communities to diversify energy purchases to reduce costs over the long-term.

Infrastructure Upgrade, Inc.® strongly supports utility bundling and energy buying cooperatives (purchasing renewable energy credits from a reliable energy marketplace) as a mechanism for increasing competition in the marketplace. In essence, purchasing companies are creating competition in the marketplace, forcing utilities to develop more energy capacity over the long-term. The private equity and venture capital community has invested in renewable energy in the past and should continue to do so.

Smart Grid Adoption

The adoption of a smart digital electric grid that provides a rapid response time for blackouts and other network outages is a strategy that is worth pursuing. Michael Grunwald in his August 6, 2012 TIME® article entitled *Rise of the Smart Grid* notes that proposals have been made "for a digital and smart grid that would self-monitor and self-heal, minimizing costly outages by diagnosing problems electronically and rerouting power around them."[65] In 2017 the industry continues to push toward a smart grid, but adoption has been fragmented in the marketplace.

Smart grid systems are particularly vulnerable to hackers both within and outside of the U.S., creating a high level of risk for nuclear reactors in particular. The security issues associated with broad smart grid adoption, coupled with consumer privacy issues have to be resolved.

The benefits of a smart grid will not outweigh the potential for civilian casualties from a reactor meltdown from a hacker infiltrating a reactor's cooling system.

---

[65]Michael Grunwald. *Rise of the Smart Grid*. TIME. July 26, 2012.

A whole industry has developed around smart grid technologies. Companies like Siemens®, Intel® and other corporations are betting that this market will explode. They are correct in their analysis. Without question chip makers and infrastructure technology providers will continue to build entire divisions around this segment. Government regulation is particularly important to the development of this sector. Public safety issues are key and corporations should expect heavy government and military intervention in this sector.

The Unites States government should form a partnership with the large regulated electric utilities and private sector to produce a more dynamic and responsive electric utility grid.

Public and Financial Planning for Large Scale Rail Projects and
Their Potential Impact on Operational Success

The California rail system was originally projected to cost almost $100 billion.[66] The current estimated cost in 2017 is still in line with the 2012 figures at $64 billion.[67]

Will the revised plan be as effective at providing a cost effective alternative to car, air or boat travel? Or did planners design a system that failed to find cost savings in unexpected areas of the initial phases of the proposal?

At the existing level traditional commuter and subway systems are tired, heavily warn and in need of repair. Rail pilings are often compressed splintered and disintegrating.

Steel on steel systems do break down. They have a structural life and new track needs to be added over the course of the systems lifetime. In New York City the subway system is overcrowded, and the track, lighting, signals and structural framework require repairs.

---

[66]*California Trims Rail Cost. The Wall Street Journal.* 2012.
[67]Katy Murphy. Confidential report: California bullet train could cost billions more than expected. The Mercury News. January 13, 2017.

Connecting two major transportation centers will have a significant impact, stimulating not just construction and growth, but new ideas, technologies and other innovations. The investment (in real dollars) now will be less than in the future and worth every penny.

I have had the privilege of living/visiting a large part of the world. I've been empowered by diversity - not weakened. Technologies like the Hyperloop One® and high-speed rail in California will strengthen communities not undermine them. The Hyperloop One® has the potential to connect whole continents, not divide them. It is worth noting that there are always costs and benefits associated with new construction, design and innovation. Nothing is perfect, but the long-term benefits of an efficient and streamlined society are exceptional.

The investment community, including individual and corporate venture capital and private equity need to partner with government to finance innovative transportation and technology. This can include new types of propulsion systems, materials, nano-technologies (coatings) and other energy innovations.

Innovative Building Design

New construction and public works projects developed in partnership with government and private developers that include innovative architectural design and/or the retrofitting and renovation of existing buildings to incorporate energy saving features, can result in the reduction of design, construction and operation costs.

Utilization of reflective (heat transfer prevention) films and coatings on glass surfaces on residential and commercial buildings can result in an energy efficiency improvements and components. Modern spray adhesives can be used to coat the glass exteriors of modern high-rise buildings and other structures that contain large glass surface areas and reduce heat flow from the outside environment into a building. For example, adding skylights (with reflective glass coatings) natural ventilation, fans for air circulation and lighting features (adding new windows to allow light, but not heat in).

Replacing (or renovating) an existing roof to include modern thermal insulation, white reflective coatings and other heat reducing features can result in energy savings for areas with intense year round sunlight. The Energy Star® website developed by the EPA and Energy Star® provides a case study in which the organization cites the following Case Study:

> Texas Cool Roof Yields Big Savings at Target®: Installing a reflective roof membrane on a 100,000-square-foot Target retail store in Austin, Texas, reduced the average summer daily maximum roof-surface temperature from 168° to 126° Fahrenheit. This temperature reduction cut the building's total air-conditioning energy use by 11 percent and peak air-conditioning demand by 14 percent. Researchers at Lawrence Berkeley National Laboratory estimate that this cool roof installation will save about $65,000 over the course of its useful life. According to the building manager, the difference in labor and materials costs for installing a white thermoplastic roof instead of a black rubber roof was negligible, so that the payback for this system was immediate.[68]

---

[68] *Reducing Supplement Loads.* Energy Star Building Manual. EPA. Revised August 2007.

For buildings located in areas with an extended winter climate retrofitting a building with additional insulation and window and door barrier guards can result in a lower heating bill (windows and doors typically are areas where heat escapes). Additionally, modifying a building with state of the art insulation can result in a significant energy savings.

Adding green roofs to a commercial (and residential building – if possible) can improve the cooling of a facility, structure or building. A green roof is simply a structure that contains plantings that provide a layer of insulation and reduce the amount of heat that is absorbed by both the roof and the building. Utilizing a green roof has the potential to result in significant energy savings, particularly in the area of electricity usage for air conditioning systems.

It is also recommended that the addition of plantings (and other features that encompass a green roof installation) be followed by the addition of photovoltaic, wind installations and rainwater re-use and recycling features.

A green roof is shown near Lakeville, Connecticut.

Designing a green roof results in immediate bottom-line savings for the individual, school, and corporation adopting this feature. It costs less to air-condition the structure over the long-term because the earth naturally absorbs the heat.

Utilization of photovoltaic canopies for parking lots to reduce radiant heat and generate electricity to power a building's operation, through a negotiated power purchase agreement with a specific large-scale utility.

The removal of lead based paint and asbestos by a licensed contractor is critical to the retrofit and renovation of buildings utilized by public and private developers, particularly those built prior to 1978 (with respect to lead), and prior to 1970 (with respect to asbestos). Specifically, the National Cancer Institute® at the National Institutes of Health® notes the following:

> In the late 1970s, the U.S. Consumer Product Safety Commission (CPSC) banned the use of asbestos in wallboard patching compounds and gas fireplaces because the asbestos fibers in these products could be released into the environment during use.[69]

---

[69]Asbestos Exposure and Cancer Risk. National Cancer Institute. 2017. https://www.cancer.gov/about-cancer/causes-prevention/risk/substances/asbestos/asbestos-fact-sheet.

Water usage can be reduced in innovative building construction and renovation projects by exterior rainwater collection systems for irrigation (the incorporation of drainage swales), and the integration of water saving residential and commercial appliances. Private equity, venture capital and corporate research can be used to find and fund alternative technologies to limit fire exposure without creating toxic by-products. Bell Labs® provided this role. Other corporations can create similar mechanisms.

Many corporations and government agencies are beginning to recognize that many modern building materials contain chemicals in construction materials, carpeting and furniture that result in significant off-gassing.

Paints, carpet, and composite furniture create significant off-gassing impact indoor buildings and environments. A similar comparison can be made to oil primer drying on a wall.

The VOCs depending on ventilation take a certain amount of time to dissipate. The same is true for composite kitchens, office furniture and building materials. Although the off-gassing is not as strong as oil primer paint these materials create a significant amount of off-gassing that can impact occupants health.

Reduced productivity and an increased number of employee sick days has been linked to this off gassing. Infrastructure Upgrade, Inc.® recommends that private corporations and government agencies, when they replace these materials that they purchase those with wools, recycled wood and metal products that do not result in significant off-gassing and have the potential to reduce the number of sick days that employees experience, a significant cost to industry and government.

Designing new facilities (or retrofitting exist ones) with gymnasiums, shower facilities and other fitness oriented features (bicycle accommodations) to improve worker productivity, reduce employer's health benefit costs and reduce the number of employee sick days.

Research is beginning to show a correlation between improved workplace efficiency and yield and on-site exercise. Buildings that contribute to a work force that is physically fit can improve the bottom-line for corporations, industry, not-for-profits and government. Housing that incorporates these features, regardless of whether it falls on the luxury end of the spectrum or is designed for low- and moderate-income persons, can result in the reduction of the medical costs to employers, the expense of providing social services by the government and improving the overall health and well being of communities. The recommended course of action is: Retrofitting buildings when possible to incorporate these features.

Other innovations in building design include the integration of Americans with Disabilities (ADA) compliant facilities, walkways, elevators, restrooms, doors, lighting and other ergonomic features to the extent feasible. Some buildings are easier than others to retrofit.

The New York Subway System drilled into bedrock consists of schist, granite and other types of rock that are very difficult to penetrate with excavation equipment, making ADA compliance very challenging. However, even in the most difficult circumstances a strategy must be developed with corresponding funding to ensure that retrofits are implemented. There is a huge difference between the Metropolitan Transit Authority (MTA) of New York attempting to add ADA compliant elevators and stairs to existing stations and the City of San Francisco adding surface level ADA compliant sidewalks and curbs. Boring and excavating through solid bedrock to add an ADA compliant elevator in New York is far more expensive and complicated that installing surface level retrofits.

Ground level modifications that include ADA compliant panels cast in the sidewalk (for the visually impaired) and the correct slope from the sidewalk into the roadway (for those individuals confined to a wheelchair or other device). These are relatively easy installations.

ADA compliant bridge additions are much more difficult to integrate (as evidenced by the Oʻahu roadway) are the example of a *non* ADA compliant site, which is six (6) thousand miles away from New York on the Island of Oʻahu, Hawaiʻi. A community that has diversity can draw upon these strengths for problem solving, approaching issues from a unique unanticipated perspective.

ADA compliancy issues and installations are shown on Oʻahu, Hawaiʻi and San Francisco, California.

The use of Energy Star® labeled computers, printers, appliances and other fixtures is a simple and cost-effective means of innovating and/or retrofitting a buildings design to be more cost effective. Energy Star® appliances can reduce the cost of utility bills, freeing up those resources towards improving a company's bottom-line and profitability.

The addition of external landscaping features for shading and drainage swales to collect runoff (where applicable) and native plantings, particularly in areas that are seasonally dry and/or have experienced droughts is a critical policy. The western United States can benefit from this strategy in particular. Areas throughout California have experienced extraordinarily high levels of drought and long-term impacts to the watershed.

Solar water (passive) heating is a standard installation for residential homes and other installations that can utilize passive heating. Highly sunny climates are perfect locations for passive solar heating (including but not limited to Texas, Hawai'i and California).

New building construction can utilize recycled materials. Hardwood flooring from bowling alleys, commercial properties, homes that are being renovated, cabinets and counters from a bar and grill that is being closed can be repurposed. These are items that take up unnecessary landfill space and are very re-usable.

The structural framework of an old house is usually excellent, utilizing real plaster, lath and hardwood flooring. The transformation of the Connecticut house is shown below. The hardwood floor in the Great room is original Connecticut old growth oak. A piece of newspaper from 1936 was found used as a spacing wedge in the renovation.

The photos below show the transformation. All materials are the original plaster and flooring. From a building perspective the quality of the materials is higher and less costly than modern sheet rock or redoing the original plaster. Old growth Connecticut timber is not commercially available any more.

The modern equivalent of non-knotty narrow grain old growth hardwood flooring is not obtainable. High quality U.S. timber or exotic milled flooring hardwoods from overseas are sourced at incredible cost to the residential or commercial buyer. Re-purposing the existing structures' core strengths is cost effective reducing a project's footprint on society at large, while delivering a more cost-effective redesign for the developer and shareholders (where applicable).

At large-scale, commercial developers can renovate existing residential and commercial structures in hard-hit communities like Detroit, creating housing that is both affordable, cost-effective and efficiently delivered. Modern construction is not the same and typically uses inexpensive carpeting, pressboard composite kitchen cabinets, composite flooring and low-cost building materials.

What is the impact of this type of suburban housing construction? Less expensive cabinets and carpeting (including emitting volatile organic compounds - VOCs) wear out more quickly and are more expensive over the short-term, creating costly future repairs. Over the long-term the use of the core features (framing, walls and flooring) of a commercial or residential structure is ideal.

The recent renovation of a Connecticut structure provides a perfect example of the strength and quality of old construction. It's true across regions and demographics. My parents were one of the first families to renovate a loft in Soho, documenting loft living in Soho for New York Magazine®.

The buildings that were renovated in the area were not legally zoned for residential use, but through lease agreements and other title issue resolutions became legal for residential use.

Today they stand as one of the most influential experiments in housing and design, to the extent that developers replicate the loft experience in new construction and market this style of living as a selling point. The factory floor that they renovated was nearly 4,000 square feet in size. Imagine using a belt sander to renovate the hardwood floors! I was not directly involved in this project; I was too young at 3. However, the influence of this project was reflected in future projects that I would work with my family on.

71 Greene Street, Manhattan, New York, NY.

Our family then moved to upstate New York, renovating a Colonial house, barn and shed, which served as my father's lab and studio for commercial photography and corporate communications strategy.

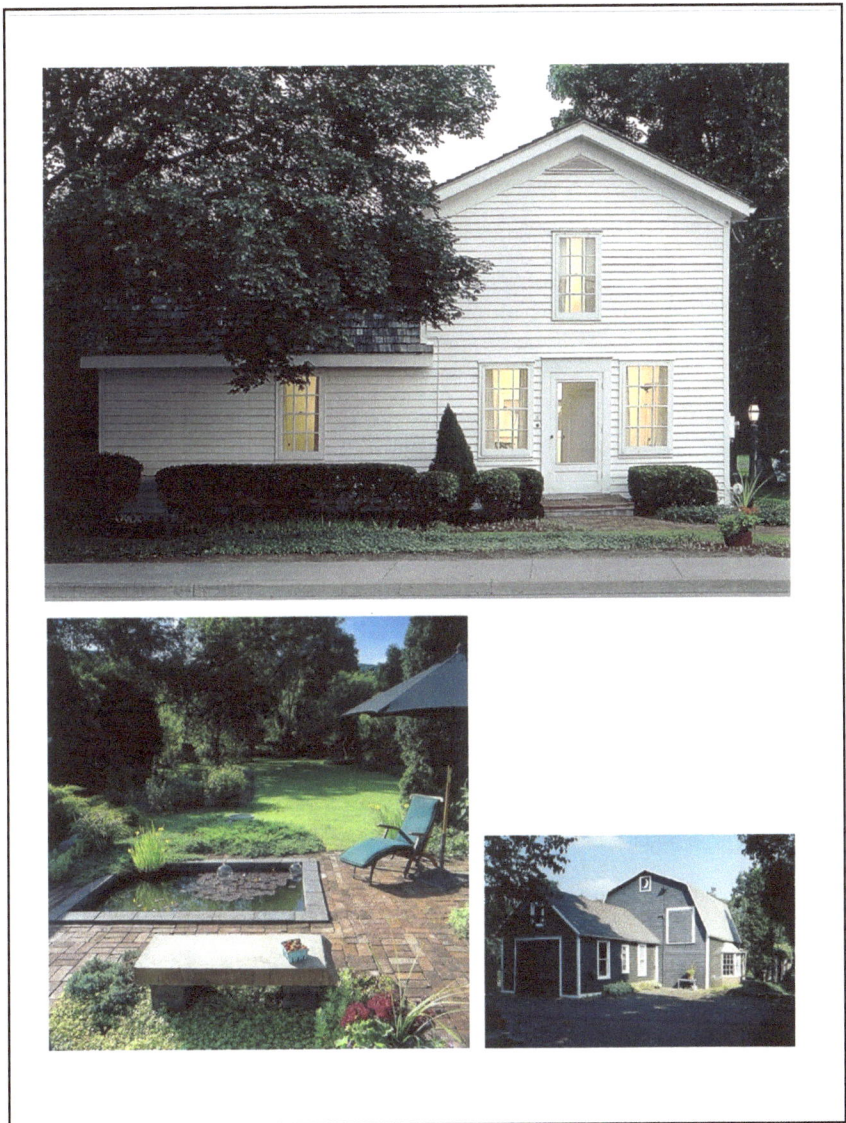

Almond, New York residence.

Included is a photo of the interior of my father's studio in Almond, New York. Growing up I was sent on assignment with him to Buffalo, Rochester and Corning, New York to assist my father in providing photo consulting services to companies including Eastman Kodak®, Corning, Inc.® and a multitude of others.

Almond, New York Stephen S. Myers Large Format Photo Studio. Photo credit: Steve S. Myers.

Years later we moved to Oʻahu, Hawaiʻi renovating a mid-1960s suburban house and lot. For this house we utilized the existing redwood lanai boards, concrete floors, shutters, louvers and jalousies, and other core features of the house designed for tropical architecture. This was in the first development on the Windward side of Oʻahu with double walled construction on concrete in lieu of elevated (or stilt) housing.

Hawaiʻi house renovation during its completion phase.

Property Right of Way Property Evolution

So what is one of the core issues behind right-of-way issues and property subdivision? Many properties that I have lived on were originally farms. The properties were sold off as families moved to urban centers, stopped farming, consolidated their operations or for any other myriad of issues. This creates a unique evolution for each of the properties and challenges for entry and exit as new roads are added to reach subdivided parcels.

Nine years later I moved to California and restored a Ranch house on nearly two acres in Fair Oaks, California. In California one of the critical development issues in urban and rural areas involves the right-of-way and access. In the Fair Oaks, California property it was challenged by a right of way road that transgressed through the middle of it.

The problem with this property was that the use of this easement road shifted over time. A church began using a property immediately below this residence for their services (illegally) – a commercial use in a residential area, without obtaining permits, conducting traffic studies or measuring the impacts on the surrounding neighbors.

Subdivision of larger tracts of property for rural, urban, commercial and industrial uses is one of the paramount challenges for developers and underwriters. How do you successfully incorporate existing properties and safely accommodate increased traffic in areas that previously did not have it? This will continue to present a challenge to the residential and commercial real estate industry. The companies and developers that can successfully address the right-of-way issue successful will emerge as the distinct corporate leaders, generating the best housing and commercial property portfolios.

Why is the case? Residents and tenants require safe and efficient access to their homes and businesses. Right-of-way access onto highways (regardless of zoning) that is poorly done impacts the financial bottom-line. Visitors are less likely to visit a mall or downtown main street business if pedestrian or vehicular access is difficult or problematic. In these cases the volume of motor vehicular and pedestrian traffic on these properties is at odds with the original design and physical dimensions of property (i.e. farm). This creates safety issues that impact the long-term economic viability of the property. As it becomes more difficult to access a property, consumers then shift their buying habits to other retail locations.

This reduces pedestrian traffic and impacts these businesses directly because consumers are less likely to visit stores and purchase merchandise or services (coffee, dry cleaning and meals).

On the residential side people are likely to sell their homes (or not purchase new ones) if right-of-way issues create significant challenges to getting to work, entering or leaving their property. For example, when I lived in upstate New York, as the main street increased traffic from gravel mining operations, noise, dust and road access (entering the road itself via car) became increasingly challenging and dangerous.

Restoration of the Fair Oaks, California estate on nearly two acres.

Now we are renovating a Connecticut house, barn, gazebo, garage, shed and studio on two acres in Connecticut (shown below). This property was originally a farm that encompassed a substantial acreage, being reduced to two acres over the long-term.

Connecticut house remodeling, including various stages of its progress.

Hydrocote Co Inc.® Polyshield Clear Superpoly®[70] is a phenomenal product, which my father stumbled upon through trial and error. It has a low emission rate and is a water-based product.

---

[70]Please note this is *not* a paid endorsement of Hydrocote Co Inc.® and/or Polyshield Clear Superpoly®. It is simply a preferred product based on low VOCs, environmental standards and ease of application.

Re-Use Hawaii is an excellent source of recycled building material. For home-construction projects in Hawai'i, California, New York, New York City and Connecticut my family has re-appropriated building materials with great success, using a combination of Japanese hand tools, English planes, rasps, and power tools to remake the building architecture into splendid structures.

For the Lanai in Hawai'i a mortise joint technique was used to join the wood for the screens (shown below) and the railing itself, creating an appearance like a Japanese temple, and using no nails or screws. Construction waste can be ground up into mulch, sawdust or pulverized for re-use, again diverting material from a landfill. As an example, the landfill in Buncombe County, NC utilizes lumber (including non-painted pallets) for mulch and biofuel.

Building design can utilize paints and other chemical applications that are non-Volatile Organic Compound (VOC) emitting treatments and coatings, improving the Indoor Air Quality (IAQ) of the facility.

Low VOC paint – pre-mixing is shown above.

For new residential projects, utilizing a detached garage with improved ventilation (space permitting) can improve a project's footprint.

Polished concrete floors (or bamboo and/or stone tile) in lieu of carpeting or other synthetic surface coverings can save money and reduce the amount of VOC's that are circulating in a building.

In the Hawai'i house the carpet was removed and replaced with polished and painted black epoxy concrete with a clear sealant.

The concrete was a part of the original structure's construction in the early 70s. The floor is easy to clean and removes toxic carpeting, significantly improving health within the structure. Carpeting is very expensive per square foot, reducing the overall maintenance costs.

Using recycled repurposed materials saves energy. It costs an extraordinary amount of energy to mill lumber; and then to ship, transport (train and truck) and distribute it to a hardware store or warehouse. Incorporating recycled materials at large-scale to reduce the energy footprint significantly. Housing or commercial warehouse renovation costs less as a consequence. These savings are returned to businesses or shareholders as a consequence.

Hawai'i house interior design at its completion phase.

Designing open ceilings and utilizing recycled joist beams can improve circulation and has the potential to reduce air conditioning costs if combined with fans and other natural ventilation systems. Drop ceilings are easy to remove in warehouses, houses or other structures and reveal the actual core-building framework. Painting these items creates a natural, open appearance that is positive for residents or employees.

Sites that are contaminated with lead can utilize ground-up fish cartilage and bone (sold by the pound) to chemically convert lead contaminated soil with the intent of re-utilizing a dormant construction site.

On-demand water heaters can be installed or used to replace existing hot water heaters (tanks) that are less efficient and require greater electricity usage.

Adding Compact florescent lamps (CFLs) and other energy efficient fixtures can improve the electricity bill of a commercial or residential building significantly.

For residential structures re-designing the framing structures to utilize fewer boards and/or utilizing steel framing in lieu of wood is an excellent cost-savings initiative.

The U.S. Green Building Council's Leadership in Energy and Environmental Design (LEED®) is a green building certification program. The program's limitation is that it adds an additional layer of expense to a residential and/or commercial project.

However, many organizations may want this certification as a mechanism for justifying the added cost of incorporating more expensive features in a building up-front with payback periods that may occur over several years.

Finding and exploiting savings and operational efficiencies in any endeavor is not environmentalism. It is good business. So often it is mislabeled as a detrimental to industry and corporations. The exact opposite is true. Energy saving initatives create growth because companies have more money to re-invest in their businesses; and return those profits to shareholders.

Fashion and Design Influencing Architecture; Revenue Impact Gains

Fashion and architecture have influenced design in a great number of areas. An examination of many modern architects reveals the influence of origami. Origami, the Japanese art of folding paper is one example of this. I have included a photo of a lobster, the first piece of origami that I learned to fold (from a museum curator friend). It is non-traditional in the sense that it involves using scissors rather than a square or rectangular piece of paper.

A red lobster origami is shown above illustrating how design can influence architecture.

It is easy to see the application of paper folding into architecture. In the lobster's tail the folds of the paper represent the roof or armature of the structure. The Sydney Opera house in New South Wales, Australia is the most striking example. It has the appearance of the lobster's tail. Paper and fabric can influence building design and vise versa.

Clothing and fabric have also influenced architectural and infrastructure design. In some cases fabric with synthetic resins like fiberglass or other nano-materials or coatings have been used directly on fabric.

Pioneering building design improves workplace potential, creating spaces that direct impact employee productivity, stimulating invention and improving the bottom line. An original workplace reduces workplace sickness, fatigue and lost-productivity, resulting in billions of dollars of revenue and bottom-line gains. To suggest otherwise, as many conservative money-managers and activist investors do in the interest of short-term stock gains, is counterintuitive. The long-term revenue gains from an innovative workplace are reflected in monetary gains that are recaptured by an increase in profitability and dividends (or stock price), in lieu of a stock buyback to improve price-earnings ratio (P/E) ratio or other metrics.

Conclusion

If one can't build a company that doesn't negatively impact the communities that surround it, you shouldn't build it. Technology and infrastructure needs to serve the public. There is never a utopia, but societies can benefit from planning and execution to build the communities and cities of the future.

www.ingramcontent.com/pod-product-compliance
Lightning Source LLC
Chambersburg PA
CBHW041313210326
41599CB00008B/255